INTERNATIONAL Y0-BEI-160

EDITED BY EDMOND R. BROWN

FIVE MODERN PLAYS

INTERNATIONAL : POCKET : LIBRARY

Other Titles in Preparation

FIVE MODERN PLAYS

THE DREAMY KID
BY EUGENE O'NEILL

THE FAREWELL SUPPER
BY ARTHUR SCHNITZLER

THE LOST SILK HAT
BY LORD DUNSANY

THE SISTERS' TRAGEDY
BY RICHARD HUGHES

THE INTRUDER
BY MAURICE MAETERLINCK

BOSTON
INTERNATIONAL POCKET LIBRARY

First Printing, 5000 copies
Second Printing, 5000 copies
Third Printing, 10,000 copies
Fourth Printing, 5000 copies

Lithographed in U.S.A. by
E D W A R D S   B R O T H E R S ,   I N C .
Ann Arbor, Michigan

THE DREAMY KID

A Play in One Act

(1918)

BY

EUGENE O'NEILL

CHARACTERS

Mammy Saunders
Abe, *her grandson, "The Dreamy Kid"*
Ceely Ann
Irene

SCENE—MAMMY SAUNDERS' *bedroom in a house just off of Carmine Street, New York City. The left of the room, forward, is taken up by a heavy, old-fashioned wooden bedstead with a feather mattress. A gaudy red-and-yellow quilt covers the other bedclothes. In back of the bed, a chest of drawers placed against the left wall. On top of the chest, a small lamp. A rocking-chair stands beside the head of the bed on the right. In the rear wall, toward the right, a low window with ragged white curtains. In the right corner, a washstand with bowl and pitcher. Bottles of medicine, a spoon, a glass, etc., are also on the stand. Farther forward, a door opening on the hall and stairway.*

It is soon after nightfall of a day in early winter. The room is in shadowy half darkness, the only light being a pale glow that seeps through the window from the arc lamp on the nearby corner, and by which the objects in the room can be dimly discerned. The vague outlines of MAMMY SAUNDERS' *figure lying in the bed can be seen, and her black face stands out in sharp contrast from the pillows that support her head.*

MAMMY [*weakly*]. Ceely Ann! [*With faint querulousness*] Light de lamp, will you? Hit's mighty dark in yere. [*After a slight pause*] Ain't you dar, Ceely Ann? [*Receiving no reply she sighs deeply and her limbs move uneasily under the bedclothes. The door is opened and shut and the stooping form of another colored woman appears in the semi-darkness. She goes to the foot of the bed sobbing softly, and stands there evidently making an effort to control her emotion.*]

MAMMY. Dat you, Ceely Ann?

CEELY [*huskily*]. Hit ain't no yuther, Mammy.

MAMMY. Light de lamp, den. I can't see nowhars.

7

CEELY. Des one second till I finds a match. [*She wipes her eyes with her handkerchief—then goes to the chest of drawers and feels around on the top of it—pretending to grumble.*] Hit beat all how dem pesky little sticks done hide umse'fs. Shoo! Yere dey is. [*She fumbles with the lamp*].

MAMMY [*suspiciously*]. You ain't been cryin', is you?

CEELY [*with feigned astonishment*]. Cryin'? I clar' ter goodness you does git de mos' fool notions lyin' dar.

MAMMY [*in a tone of relief*]. I mos' thought I yeard you.

CEELY [*lighting the lamp*]. 'Deed you ain't. [*The two women are revealed by the light. MAMMY SAUNDERS is an old, white-haired negress about ninety with a weazened face furrowed by wrinkles and withered by old age and sickness. CEELY is a stout woman of fifty or so with gray hair and a round fat face. She wears a loose-fitting gingham dress and a shawl thrown over her head.*]

CEELY [*with attempted cheeriness*]. Bless yo' soul, I ain't got nothin' to cry 'bout. Yere. Lemme fix you so you'll rest mo' easy. [*She lifts the old woman gently and fixes the pillows*]. Dere. Now, ain't you feelin' better?

MAMMY [*dully*]. My strenk done all went. I can't lift a hand.

CEELY [*hurriedly*]. Dat'll all come back ter you de doctor tole me des now when I goes down to de door with him. [*Glibly*]. He say you is de mos' strongest 'oman fo' yo' years ever he sees in de worl'; and he tell me you gwine ter be up and walkin' agin fo' de week's out. [*As she finds the old woman's eyes fixed on her she turns away confusedly and abruptly changes the subject*]. Hit ain't too wa'm in dis room, dat's a fac'.

MAMMY [*shaking her head—in a half whisper*]. No, Ceely Ann. Hit ain't no use'n you tellin' me nothin' but de trufe. I feels mighty poo'ly. En I knows hit's on'y wid de blessin' er God I kin las' de night out.

CEELY [*distractedly*]. Ain't no sich a thing! Hush yo' noise, Mammy!

MAMMY [*as if she hadn't heard—in a crooning singsong*]. I'se gwine soon fum dis wicked yearth—and may de Lawd have mercy on dis po' ole sinner. [*After a pause—anxiously*]. All I'se prayin' fer is dat God don' take me befo' I sees Dreamy agin. Whar's Dreamy, Ceely Ann? Why ain't he come yere? Ain't you done sent him word I'se sick like I tole you?

CEELY. I tole dem boys ter tell him speshul, and dey swar dey would soon's dey find him. I s'pose dey ain't kotch him yit. Don' you pester yo'se'f worryin'. Dreamy 'ull come fo' ve'y long.

MAMMY [*after a pause—weakly*]. Dere's a feelin' in my haid like I was a-floatin' yander whar I can't see nothin', or 'member nothin', or know de sight er any pusson I knows; en I wants ter see Dreamy agin befo'——

CEELY [*quickly*]. Don' waste yo' strenk talkin'. You git a wink er sleep en I wake you when he comes, you heah me?

MAMMY [*faintly*]. I does feel mighty drowsy. [*She closes her eyes.* CEELY *goes over to the window and pulling the curtains aside stands looking down into the street as if she were watching for someone coming. A moment later there is a noise of footfalls from the stairs in the hall, followed by a sharp rap on the door.*]

CEELY [*turning quickly from the window*]. Ssshh! Ssshh! [*She hurries to the door, glancing anxiously toward* MAMMY. *The old woman appears to have fallen asleep.* CEELY *cautiously opens the door a bare inch or so and peeks out. When she sees who it is she immediately tries to slam it shut again but a vigorous shove from the outside forces her back and* IRENE *pushes her way defiantly into the room. She is a young, good-looking negress, highly rouged and powdered, dressed in gaudy, cheap finery.*]

IRENE [*in a harsh voice—evidently worked up to a great state of nervous excitement*]. No you don't, Ceely Ann! I said I was comin' here and it'll take mo'n you to stop me!

CEELY [*almost speechless with horrified indignation—breathing heavily*]. Yo' bad 'oman! Git back ter yo' bad-house whar yo' b'longs!

IRENE [*raising her clenched hand—furiously*]. Stop dat talkin' to me, nigger, or I'll split yo' fool head! [*As* CEELY *shrinks away* IRENE *lowers her hand and glances quickly around the room.*] Whar's Dreamy?

CEELY [*scornfully*]. Yo' ax me dat! Whar's Dreamy? Ax yo'se'f. Yo's de one ought ter know whar he is.

IRENE. Den he ain't come here?

CEELY. I ain't tellin' de likes er you wedder he is or not.

IRENE [*pleadingly*]. Tell me, Ceely Ann, ain't he been here? He'd be sure to come here 'count of Mammy dyin', dey said.

CEELY [*pointing to* MAMMY—*apprehensively*]. Sssshh! [*Then lowering her voice to a whisper—suspiciously*] Dey said? Who said?

IRENE [*equally suspicious*]. None o' your business who said. [*Then pleading again*] Ceely Ann, I jest got ter see him dis minute, dis secon'! He's in bad, Dreamy is, and I knows somep'n I gotter tell him, somep'n I jest heard—

CEELY [*uncomprehendingly*]. In bad? What you jest heah?

IRENE. I ain't tellin' no one but him. [*Desperately*] For Gawd's sake, tell me whar he is, Ceely!

CEELY. I don' know no mo'n you.

IRENE [*fiercely*]. You's lyin', Ceely! You's lyin' ter me jest 'cause I'se bad.

CEELY. De good Lawd bar witness I'se tellin' you de trufe!

IRENE [*hopelessly*]. Den I gotter go find him, high and low, somewheres [*proudly*]. You ain't got de right not ter trust me, Ceely, where de Dreamy's mixed in it. I'd go ter hell for Dreamy!

CEELY [*indignantly*]. Hush yo' wicked cussin'! [*Then anxiously*] Is Dreamy in trouble?

IRENE [*with a scornful laugh*]. Trouble? Good Lawd, it's worser'n dat! [*Then in surprise*] Ain't you heerd what de Dreamy done last night, Ceely?

CEELY [*apprehensively*]. What de Dreamy do? Tell me, gal. Somep'n bad?

IRENE [*with the same scornful laugh*]. Bad? Worser'n bad, what he done!

CEELY [*lamenting querulously*]. Oh good Lawd, I knowed it! I knowed with all his carryin's-on wid dat passel er tough young niggers—him so uppity 'cause he's de boss er de gang—sleepin' all de day 'stead er workin' an' Lawd knows what he does in de nights—fightin' wid white folks, an' totin' a pistol in his pocket—[*with a glance of angry resentment at* IRENE]—an' as fo' de udder company he's been keepin'——

IRENE [*fiercely*]. Shut your mouth, Ceely! Dat ain't your business.

CEELY. Oh, I knowed Dreamy'd be gittin' in trouble fo' long! De lowflung young trash! An' here's his ole Mammy don' know no dif'frunt but he's de mos' innercent young lamb in de worl'. [*In a strained whisper*] What he do? Is he been stealin' somep'n?

IRENE [*angrily*] You go ter hell, Ceely Ann! You ain't no fren' of de Dreamy's, you talk dat way, and I ain't got no time ter waste argyin' wid your fool notions. [*She goes to the door.*] Dreamy'll go ter his death sho's yo' born, if I don't find him an' tell him quick!

CEELY [*terrified*]. Oh Lawd!

IRENE [*anxiously*]. He'll sho'ly try ter come here and see

his ole Mammy befo' she dies, don't you think, Ceely?

CEELY. Fo' Gawd, I hopes so! She's been a-prayin' all de day——

IRENE [*opening the door*]. You hopes so, you fool nigger! I tells you it's good-by to de Dreamy, he come here! I knows! I gotter find an' stop him. If he come here, Ceely, you tell him git out quick and hide, he don't wanter git pinched. You hear? You tell him dat, Ceely, for Gawd's sake! I'se got ter go—find him—high an' low. [*She goes out leaving* CEELY *staring at her in speechless indignation*].

CEELY [*drawing a deep breath*]. Yo' street gal! I don' b'lieve one word you says—stuffin' me wid yo' bad lies so's you kin keep de Dreamy frum leavin' you. [MAMMY SAUNDERS *awakes and groans faintly*. CEELY *hurries over to her bedside*.] Is de pain hurtin' again, Mammy?

MAMMY [*vaguely*]. Dat you, Dreamy?

CEELY. No, Mammy, dis is Ceely. Dreamy's comin' soon. Is you restin' easy?

MAMMY [*as if she hadn't heard*]. Dat you, Dreamy?

CEELY [*sitting down in the rocker by the bed and taking one of the old woman's hands in hers*]. No. Dreamy's comin'.

MAMMY [*after a pause—suddenly*]. Does you 'member yo' dead Mammy, chile?

CEELY [*mystified*]. My dead Mammy?

MAMMY. Didn' I heah yo' talkin' jest now, Dreamy?

CEELY [*very worried*]. I clar ter goodness, she don' know me ary bit. Dis is Ceely Ann talkin' ter yo', Mammy.

MAMMY. Who was yo' talkin' wid, Dreamy?

CEELY [*shaking her head—in a trembling voice*]. Hit can't be long befo' de en'. [*In a louder tone*] Hit was me talkin' wid a pusson fum ovah de way. She say tell you Dreamy comin' heah ter see yo' right away. You heah dat, Mammy? [*The old woman sighs but does not answer. There is a pause.*]

MAMMY [*suddenly*]. Does yo' 'member yo' dead Mammy, chile? [*Then with a burst of religious exaltation*] De Lawd have mercy!

CEELY [*like an echo*]. Bless de Lawd! [*Then in a frightened half-whisper to herself*] Po' thing! Her min's done leavin' her jest like de doctor said. [*She looks down at the old woman helplessly. The door on the right is opened stealthily and* THE DREAMY KID *slinks in on tiptoe.*]

CEELY [*hearing a board creak, turns quickly toward the door and gives a frightened start*]. Dreamy!

DREAMY [*puts his fingers to his lips—commandingly*]. Sshh! [*He bends down to a crouching position and holding the door about an inch open, peers out into the hallway in an attitude of tense waiting, one hand evidently clutching some weapon in the side pocket of his coat. After a moment he is satisfied of not being followed, and, after closing the door carefully and locking it, he stands up and walks to the center of the room casting a look of awed curiosity at the figure in the bed. He is a well-built, good-looking young negro, light in color. His eyes are shifty and hard, their expression one of tough, scornful defiance. His mouth is cruel and perpetually drawn back at the corners into a snarl. He is dressed in well-fitting clothes of a flashy pattern. A light cap is pulled down on the side of his head.*]

CEELY [*coming from the bed to meet him*]. Bless de Lawd, here you is at las'!

DREAMY [*with a warning gesture*]. Nix on de loud talk! Talk low, can't yuh! [*He glances back at the door furtively—then continues with a sneer*] Yuh're a fine nut, Ceely Ann! What for you sendin' out all ober de town for me like you was crazy! D'you want ter git me in de cooler? Don' you know dey're after me for what I done last night?

CEELY [*fearfully*]. I heerd somep'n—but—what you done, Dreamy?

DREAMY [*with an attempt at a careless bravado*]. I croaked a guy, dat's what! A white man.

CEELY [*in a frightened whisper*]. What you mean—croaked?

DREAMY [*boastfully*]. I shot him dead, dat's what! [*As CEELY shrinks away from him in horror—resentfully*] Aw say, don' gimme none o' dem looks o' yourn. 'T'warn't my doin' nohow. He was de one lookin' for trouble. I wasn't seekin' for no mess wid him dat I could help. But he told folks he was gwine ter git me for a fac', and dat fo'ced my hand. I had ter git him ter pertect my own life. [*With cruel satisfaction*] And I got him right, you b'lieve me!

CEELY [*putting her hands over her face with a low moan of terror*]. May de good Lawd pardon yo' wickedness! Oh Lawd! What yo' po' ole Mammy gwine say if she hear tell —an' she never knowin' how bad you's got.

DREAMY [*fiercely*]. Hell! You ain't tole her, is you?

CEELY. Think I want ter kill her on de instant? An' I didn' know myse'f—what you done—till you tells me. [*Frightenedly*] Oh, Dreamy, what you gwine do now? How you gwine git away? [*Almost wailing*] Good Lawd, de perlice gon' kotch you suah!

DREAMY [*savagely*] Shut yo' loud mouth, damn you! [*He stands tensely listening for some sound from the hall. After a moment he points to the bed.*] Is Mammy sleepin'?

CEELY [*tiptoes to the bed*]. Seems like she is. [*She comes back to him.*] Dat's de way wid her—sleep fo' a few minutes, den she wake, den sleep again.

DREAMY [*scornfully*]. Aw, dere ain't nothin' wrong wid her 'ceptin' she's ole. What yuh wanter send de word tellin' me she's croakin', and git me comin' here at de risk o' my life, and den find her sleepin'? [*Clenching his fist threateningly*] I gotter mind ter smash yo' face for playin' de damn fool and makin' me de goat. [*He turns toward the door.*] Ain't no use'n me stayin' here when dey'll likely come lookin' for me. I'm gwine out where I gotta chance ter make my git-away. De boys is all fixin' it up for me. [*His hand on the doorknob*] When Mammy wakes, you tell her I couldn't wait, you hear?

CEELY [*hurrying to him and grabbing his arm—pleadingly*]. Don' yo' go now, Dreamy—not jest yit. Fo' de good Lawd's sake, don' you go befo' you speaks wid her! If yo' knew how she's been a-callin' an' a-prayin' fo' yo' all de day——

DREAMY [*scornfully but a bit uncertainly*]. Aw, she don' need none o' me. What good kin I do watchin' her do a kip? It'd be dif'frunt if she was croakin' on de level.

CEELY [*in an anguished whisper*]. She's gwine wake up in a secon' an' den she call: "Dreamy. Whar's Dreamy?" —an' what I gwine tell her den? An' yo' Mammy is dyin', Dreamy, sho's fate! Her min' been wanderin' an' she don' even recernize me no mo', an' de doctor say when dat come it ain't but a sho't time befo' de en'. Yo' gotter stay wid yo' Mammy long 'nuff ter speak wid her, Dreamy. Yo' jest gotter stay wid her in her las' secon's on dis yearth when she's callin' ter yo'. [*With conviction as he hesitates*] Listen heah, yo' Dreamy! Yo' don' never git no bit er luck in dis worril ary agin, yo' leaves her now. De perlice gon' kotch yo' suah.

DREAMY [*with superstitious fear*]. Ssshh! Can dat bull, Ceely! [*Then boastfully*] I wasn't pinin' to beat it up here, git me? De boys was all persuadin' me not ter take de chance. It's takin' my life in my hands, dat's what. But when I heerd it was ole Mammy croakin' and axin' ter see me, I says ter myse'f: "Dreamy, you gotter make good wid old Mammy no matter what come—or you don' never git a bit of luck in yo' life no mo'." And I was game and come, wasn't I? Nary body in dis worril kin say de Dreamy ain't game ter de core, n'matter what. [*With sudden decision walks to the foot of the bed and stands looking down at* MAMMY. *A note of fear creeps into his voice.*] Gawd, she's quiet 'nuff. Maybe she done passed away in her sleep like de ole ones does. You go see, Ceely; an' if she's on'y sleepin', you wake her up. I wanter speak wid her quick—an' den I'll make a break outa here. You make it fast, Ceely Ann, I tells yo'.

CEELY [*bends down beside the bed*]. Mammy! Mammy! Here's de Dreamy.

MAMMY [*opens her eyes—drowsily and vaguely, in a weak voice*]. Dreamy?

DREAMY [*shuffling his feet and moving around the bed*]. Here I is, Mammy.

MAMMY [*fastening her eyes on him with fascinated joy*]. Dreamy! Hit's yo'! [*Then uncertainly*] I ain't dreamin' nor seein' ha'nts, is I?

DREAMY [*coming forward and taking her hand*]. 'Deed I ain't no ghost. Here I is, sho' 'nuff.

MAMMY [*clutching his hand tight and pulling it down on her breast—in an ecstasy of happiness*]. Didn' I know you'd come! Didn' I say: "Dreamy ain't gwine let his ole Mammy die all lone by he'se'f an' him not dere wid her." I knows yo'd come. [*She starts to laugh joyously, but coughs and sinks back weakly.*]

DREAMY [*shudders in spite of himself as he realizes for the first time how far gone the old woman is—forcing a tone of joking reassurance*]. What's dat foolishness I hears you talkin', Mammy? Wha' d'yuh mean pullin' dat bull 'bout croakin' on me? Shoo! Tryin' ter kid me, ain't you? Shoo! You live ter plant de flowers on my grave, see if you don'.

MAMMY [*sadly and very weakly*]. I knows! I knows! Hit ain't long now. [*Bursting into a sudden weak hysteria*] Yo' stay heah. Dreamy! Yo' stay heah by me, yo' stay heah—till de good Lawd takes me home. Yo' promise me dat! Yo' do dat fo' po' ole Mammy, won't you'?

DREAMY [*uneasily*]. 'Deed I will, Mammy, 'deed I will.

MAMMY [*closing her eyes with a sigh of relief—calmly*]. Bless de Lawd for dat. Den I ain't skeered no mo'. [*She settles herself comfortably in the bed as if preparing for sleep.*]

CEELY [*in a low voice*]. I gotter go home fo' a minute, Dreamy. I ain't been dere all de day and Lawd knows what happen. I'll be back yere befo' ve'y long.

DREAMY [*his eyes fixed on* MAMMY]. Aw right, beat it if yuh wanter. [*Turning to her—in a fierce whisper*] On'y don' be long. I can't stay here an' take dis risk, you hear?

CEELY [*frightenedly*]. I knows, chile. I come back, I swar! [*She goes out quietly.* DREAMY *goes quickly to the window and cautiously searches the street below with his eyes*].

MAMMY [*uneasily*]. Dreamy. [*He hurries back and takes her hand again.*] I got de mos' 'culiar feelin' in my head. Seems like de years done all roll away an' I'm back down home in de ole place whar you was bo'n. [*After a short pause*] Does yo' 'member yo' own mammy, chile?

DREAMY. No.

MAMMY. Yo' was too young, I s'pec'. Yo' was on'y a baby w'en she tuck 'n' die. May Sal was a mighty fine 'oman, if I does say hit m'se'f.

DREAMY [*fidgeting nervously*]. Don' you talk, Mammy. Better you'd close yo' eyes an' rest.

MAMMY [*with a trembling smile—weakly*]. Shoo! W'at is I done come ter wid my own gran' chile bossin' me 'bout? I wants ter talk. You knows you ain't give me much chance ter talk wid yo' dese las' years.

DREAMY [*sullenly*]. I ain't had de time, Mammy; but you knows I was always game ter give you anything I got.

[*A note of appeal in his voice*] You knows dat, don' you, Mammy?

MAMMY. Sho'ly I does. Yo' been a good boy, Dreamy; an' if dere's one thing more'n 'nother makes me feel like I mighter done good in de sight er de Lawd, hit's dat I raised yo' fum a baby.

DREAMY [*clearing his throat gruffly*]. Don' you talk so much, Mammy.

MAMMY [*querulously*]. I gotter talk, chile. Come times —w'en I git thinkin' yere in de bed—w'at's gwine ter come ter me a'mos' b'fore I knows hit— like de thief in de night —en den I gits skeered. But w'en I talks wid yo' I ain't skeered a bit.

DREAMY [*defiantly*]. You ain't got nothin' to be skeered of—not when de Dreamy's here.

MAMMY [*after a slight pause, faintly*]. Dere's a singin' in my ears all de time. [*Seized by a sudden religious ecstasy*] Maybe hit's de singin' hymns o' de blessed angels I done heah fum above. [*Wildly*] Bless Gawd! Bless Gawd! Pity dis po' ole sinner.

DREAMY [*with an uneasy glance at the door.*] Ssshh, Mammy! Don' shout so loud.

MAMMY. De pictures keep a whizzin' fo' my eyes like de thread in a sewing machine. Seems's if all my life done fly back ter me all ter once. [*With a flickering smile —weakly*] Does you know how yo' come by dat nickname dey alls call yo'—de Dreamy? Is I ever tole yo' dat?

DREAMY [*evidently lying*]. No, Mammy.

MAMMY. Hit was one mawnin' b'fo' we come No'th. Me an' yo' mammy—yo' was des a baby in arms den—

DREAMY [*hears a noise from the hall*]. Ssshh, Mammy! For God's sake, don't speak for a minute. I hears somep'n. [*He stares at the door, his face hardening savagely, and listens intently.*]

MAMMY [*in a frightened tone*]. W'at's de matter, chile?

DREAMY. Ssshh! Somebody comin'. [*A noise of foot-steps comes from the hall stairway.* DREAMY *springs to his feet.*] Leggo my hand, Mammy—jest for a secon'. I come right back to you. [*He pulls his hand from the old woman's grip. She falls back on the pillows moaning.* DREAMY *pulls a large automatic revolver from his coat pocket and tiptoes quickly to the door. As he does so there is a sharp rap. He stands listening at the crack for a moment, then noiselessly turns the key, unlocking the door. Then he crouches low down by the wall so that the door, when opened, will hide him from the sight of anyone entering. There is another and louder rap on the door.*]

MAMMY [*groaning*]. W'at's dat, Dreamy? Whar is yo'?

DREAMY. Ssshh! [*Then muffling his voice he calls*]: Come in. [*He raises the revolver in his hand. The door is pushed open and* IRENE *enters, her eyes peering wildly about the room. Her bosom is heaving as if she had been running and she is trembling all over with terrified excitement*].

IRENE [*not seeing him calls out questioningly*]. Dreamy?

DREAMY [*lowering his revolver and rising to his feet roughly*]. Close dat door!

IRENE [*whirling about with a startled cry*]. Dreamy!

DREAMY [*shutting the door and locking it—aggressively*]. Shut yo' big mouth, gal, or I'll bang it shut for you! You wanter let de whole block know where I is?

IRENE [*hysterical with joy—trying to put her arms around him*]. Bless God, I foun' you at last!

DREAMY [*pushing her away roughly*]. Leggo o' me! Why you come here follerin' me? Ain't yo' got 'nuff sense in yo' fool head ter know de bulls is liable ter shadow you when dey knows you's my gal? Is you pinin' ter git me kotched an' sent to de chair?

IRENE [*terrified*]. No, no!

DREAMY [*savagely*]. I gotter mind ter hand you one you won't ferget! [*He draws back his fist.*]

IRENE [*shrinking away*]. Don' you hit me, Dreamy! Don' you beat me up now! Jest lemme 'xplain, dat's all.

MAMMY [*in a frightened whimper*]. Dreamy! Come yere to me. Whar is yo'? I'se skeered!

DREAMY [*in a fierce whisper to* IRENE]. Can that bull or I'll fix you. [*He hurries to the old woman and pats her hand.*] Here I is, Mammy.

MAMMY. Who dat you's a-talkin' wid?

DREAMY. On'y a fren' o' Ceely Ann's, Mammy, askin' where she is. I gotter talk wid her some mo' yit. You sleep, Mammy? [*He goes to* IRENE].

MAMMY [*feebly*]. Don' yo' leave me, Dreamy.

DREAMY. I'se right here wid you. [*Fiercely, to* IRENE]. You git the hell outa here, you Reeny, you heah—quick! Dis ain't no place for de likes o' you wid ole Mammy dyin'.

IRENE [*with a horrified glance at the bed*]. Is she dyin' —honest?

DREAMY. Ssshh! She's croakin', I tells yo'—an' I gotter stay wid her fo' a while—an' I ain't got no time ter be pesterin' wid you. Beat it, now! Beat it outa here befo' I knocks yo' cold, git me?

IRENE. Jest wait a secon' for de love o' Gawd. I got somep'n ter tell you—

DREAMY. I don' wanter hear yo' fool talk. [*He gives her a push toward the door.*] Git outa dis, you hear me?

IRENE. I'll go. I'm going soon— soon's ever I've had my say. Lissen, Dreamy! It's about de coppers I come ter tell you.

DREAMY [*quickly*]. Why don' you say dat befo'? What you know, gal?

IRENE. Just befo' I come here to find you de first time, de Madam sends me out to Murphy's ter git her a bottle o' gin. I goes in de side door but I ain't rung de bell yet. I hear yo' name spoken an' I stops ter lissen. Dey was three or four men in de back room. Dey don't hear me open de outside door, an' dey can't see me, 'course. It was Big Sullivan from de Central Office talkin'. He was talkin' 'bout de killin' you done last night and he tells dem udders he's heerd 'bout de ole woman gittin' so sick, and dat if dey don't fin' you none of de udder places dey's lookin', dey's goin' wait for you here. Dey s'pecs you come here say good-by to Mammy befo' you make yo' gitaway.

DREAMY. It's aw right den. Dey ain't come yit. Twister Smith done tole me de coast was clear befo' I come here.

IRENE. Dat was den. It ain't now.

DREAMY [excitedly]. What you mean, gal?

IRENE. I was comin' in by de front way when I sees some pusson hidin' in de doorway 'cross de street. I gits a good peek at him and when I does—it's a copper, Dreamy, suah's yo born, in his plain close, and he's a watchin' de door o' dis house like a cat.

DREAMY. [Goes to the window and stealthily crouching by the dark side peeks out. One glance is enough. He comes quickly back to IRENE.] You got de right dope, gal. It's dat Mickey. I knows him even in de dark. Dey're waitin' —so dey ain't wise I'm here yit, dat's suah.

IRENE. But dey'll git wise befo' long.

DREAMY. He don' pipe you comin' in here?

IRENE. I skulked roun' and sneaked in by de back way froo de yard. Dey ain't none o' dem dar yit. [Raising her voice—excitedly] But dere will be soon. Dey're boun' to git wise to dat back door. You ain't got no time to lose, Dreamy. Come on wid me now. Git back where yo' safe. It's de cooler for you certain if you stays here. Dey'll git you like a rat in de trap. [As DREAMY hesitates] For de love of Gawd, Dreamy, wake up to youse'f!

DREAMY [uncertainly]. I can't beat it—wid Mammy here alone. My luck done turn bad all my life, if I does.

IRENE [*fiercely*]. What good's you gittin' pinched and sent to de chair gwine do her? Is you crazy mad? Come wid me, I tells you!

DREAMY [*half-persuaded—hesitatingly*]. I gotter speak wid her. You wait a secon'.

IRENE [*wringing her hands*]. Dis ain't no time now for fussin' wid her.

DREAMY [*gruffly*]. Shut up! [*He makes a motion for her to remain where she is and goes over to the bed—in a low voice*] Mammy.

MAMMY [*hazily*]. Dat you, Dreamy? [*She tries to reach out her hand and touch him.*]

DREAMY. I'm gwine leave you—jest for a moment, Mammy. I'll send de word for Ceely Ann—

MAMMY [*wide awake in an instant—with intense alarm*]. Don' yo' do dat! Don' yo' move one step out er yere or you'll be sorry, Dreamy.

DREAMY [*apprehensively*]. I gotter go, I tells you. I'll come back.

MAMMY [*with wild grief*]. O good Lawd! When I's drawin' de las' bre'fs in dis po' ole body—[*Frenziedly*] De Lawd have mercy! Good Lawd have mercy!

DREAMY [*fearfully*]. Stop dat racket, Mammy! You bring all o' dem down on my head! [*He rushes over and crouches by the window again to peer out—in relieved tones.*] He ain't heerd nothin'. He's dar yit.

IRENE [*imploringly*]. Come on, Dreamy! [MAMMY *groans with pain.*]

DREAMY [*hurrying to the bed*]. What's de matter, Mammy?

IRENE [*stamping her foot*]. Dreamy! Fo' Gawd's sake!

MAMMY. Lawd have mercy! [*She groans.*] Gimme yo' han', chile. Yo' ain't gwine leave me now, Dreamy? Yo' ain't, is yo'? Yo' ole Mammy won't bodder yo' long. Yo' know w'at yo' promise me, Dreamy! Yo' promise yo' sacred word yo' stay wid me till de en'. [*With an air of somber prophecy—slowly*] If yo' leave me now, yo' ain't gwine git no bit er luck s'long's yo' live, I tells yo' dat!

DREAMY [*frightened—pleadingly*]. Don' you say dat, Mammy!

IRENE. Come on, Dreamy!

DREAMY [*slowly*]. I can't. [*In awed tones*] Don' you hear de curse she puts on me if I does?

MAMMY [*her voice trembling with weak tears*]. Don't go, chile!

DREAMY [*hastily*]. I won't leave dis room, I swar ter you!
[*Relieved by the finality in his tones, the old woman sighs and closes her eyes.* DREAMY *frees his hand from hers and goes to* IRENE. *He speaks with a strange calm*] De game's up, gal. You better beat it while de goin's good.

IRENE [*aghast*]. You gwine stay?

DREAMY. I gotter, gal. I ain't gwine agin her dyin' curse. No, suh!

IRENE [*pitifully*]. But dey'll git you suah!

DREAMY [*slapping the gun in his pocket significantly*]. Dey'll have some gittin'. I git some o' dem fust. [*With gloomy determination*] Dey don't git dis chicken alive! Lawd Jesus, no suh. Not de Dreamy!

IRENE [*helplessly*]. Oh, Lawdy, Lawdy! [*She goes to the window—with a short cry.*] He's talkin' wid someone. Dere's two o' dem. [DREAMY *hurries to her side.*]

DREAMY. I knows him—de udder. It's Big Sullivan. [*Pulling her away roughly*] Come out o' dat! Dey'll see you. [*He pushes her toward the door.*] Dey won't wait down dere much longer. Dey'll be comin' up here soon. [*Prayerfully, with a glance at the bed*] I hopes she's croaked by den, 'fo Christ I does!

IRENE [*as if she couldn't believe it*]. Den you ain't

gwine save youse'f while dere's time? [*Pleadingly*] Oh, Dreamy, you can make it yit!

DREAMY. De game's up, I tole you. [*With gloomy fatalism*] I s'pect it hatter be. Yes, suh. Dey'd git me in de long run anyway—and wid her curse de luck'd be agin me. [*With sudden anger*] Git outa here, you Reeny! You ain't aimin' ter get shot up too, is you? Ain't no sense in dat.

IRENE [*fiercely*]. I'se stayin' too, here wid you!

DREAMY. No you isn't! None o' dat bull! You ain't got no mix in dis jam.

IRENE. Yes, I is! Ain't you my man?

DREAMY. Don' make no diff. I don't wanter git you in Dutch more'n you is. It's bad 'nuff fo' me. [*He pushes her toward the door.*] Blow while you kin, I tells you.

IRENE [*resisting him*]. No, Dreamy! What I care if dey kills me? I'se gwine stick wid you.

DREAMY [*gives her another push*]. No, you isn't, gal. [*Unlocking the door—relentlessly*] Out wid you!

IRENE [*hysterically*]. You can't gimme no bum's rush. I'm gwine stay.

DREAMY [*gloomily*] On'y one thing fo' me ter do den. [*He hits her on the side of the face with all his might knocking her back against the wall where she sways as if about to fall. Then he opens the door and grabs her two arms from behind.*] Out wid you, gal!

IRENE [*moaning*]. Dreamy! Dreamy! Lemme stay wid you! [*He pushes her into the hallway and holds her there at arm's length.*] Fo' Gawd's sake, Dreamy!

MAMMY [*whimperingly*]. Dreamy! I'se skeered!

IRENE [*from the hall*]. I'se gwine stay right here at de door. You might's well lemme in.

DREAMY [*frowning*]. Don' do dat, Reeny. [*Then with a sudden idea*] You run roun' and tell de gang what's up. Maybe dey git me outa dis, you hear?

IRENE [*with eager hope*]. You think dey kin?

DREAMY. Never kin tell. You hurry—through de back yard, 'member—an' don' git pinched, now.

IRENE [*eagerly*]. I'm gwine! I'll bring dem back!

DREAMY [*stands listening to her retreating footsteps—then shuts and locks the door—gloomily to himself*]. Ain't no good. Dey dassent do nothin'—but I hatter git her outa dis somehow.

MAMMY [*groaning*]. Dreamy!

DREAMY. Here I is. Jest a secon'. [*He goes to the window.*]

MAMMY [*weakly*]. I feels—like—de en's comin'. Oh, Lawd, Lawd!

DREAMY [*absent-mindedly*]. Yes, Mammy. [*Aloud to himself*] Dey're sneakin' 'cross de street. Dere's anudder of 'em. Dat's tree. [*He glances around the room quickly —then hurries over and takes hold of the chest of drawers. As he does so the old woman commences to croon shrilly to herself.*]

DREAMY. Stop dat noise, Mammy! Stop dat noise!

MAMMY [*wanderingly*]. Dat's how come yo' got dat —dat nickname—Dreamy.

DREAMY. Yes, Mammy. [*He puts the lamp on the floor to the rear of the door, turning it down low. Then he carries the chest of drawers over and places it against the door as a barricade.*]

MAMMY [*rambling as he does this—very feebly*]. Does yo' know—I give you dat name—w'en yo's des a baby— lyin' in my arms—

DREAMY. Yes, Mammy.

MAMMY. Down by de crik—under de ole willow—whar I uster take yo'—wid yo' big eyes a-chasin'—de sun flitterin' froo de grass—an' out on de water—

DREAMY [*takes the revolver from his pocket and puts it on top of the chest of drawers*]. Dey don' git de Dreamy alive—not for de chair! Lawd Jesus, no suh!

MAMMY. An' yo' was always—a-lookin'—an' a-thinkin' ter yo'self—an' yo' big eyes jest a-dreamin' an' a-dreamin' —an' dat's w'en I gives yo' dat nickname—Dreamy— Dreamy—

DREAMY. Yes, Mammy. [*He listens at the crack of the door—in a tense whisper.*] I don' hear dem—but dey're comin' sneakin' up de stairs, I knows it.

MAMMY [*faintly*]. Whar is yo', Dreamy? I can't— ha'dly—breathe—no mo'. Oh, Lawd have mercy!

DREAMY [*goes over to the bed*]. Here I is, Mammy.

MAMMY [*speaking with difficulty*]. Yo'—kneel down chile—say a pray'r—Oh, Lawd!

DREAMY. Jest a secon', Mammy. [*He goes over and gets his revolver and comes back.*]

MAMMY. Gimme—yo' hand—chile. [DREAMY *gives her his left hand. The revolver is in his right. He stares nervously at the door*] An' yo' kneel down—pray fo' me. [DREAMY *gets on one knee beside the bed. There is a sound from the hallway as if someone had made a misstep on the stairs—then silence.* DREAMY *starts and half aims his gun in the direction of the door.* MAMMY *groans weakly*] I'm dyin', chile. Hit's de en'. You pray for me —out loud—so's I can heah. Oh, Lawd! [*She gasps to catch her breath*].

DREAMY [*abstractedly, not having heard a word she has said*]. Yes, Mammy. [*Aloud to himself with an air of grim determination as if he were making a pledge*]. Dey don't git de Dreamy! Not while he's 'live! Lawd Jesus, no suh!

MAMMY [*falteringly*]. Dat's right—yo' pray—Lawd Jesus—Lawd Jesus—[*There is another slight sound of movement from the hallway.*]

[THE CURTAIN FALLS]

THE FAREWELL SUPPER

BY

ARTHUR SCHNITZLER

CHARACTERS

ANNIE
MAX
ANATOL
A WAITER

Private room at Sacher's restaurant. ANATOL *is standing by the door giving the* WAITER *his orders.* MAX *is leaning back in an armchair.*

MAX. Well, are you nearly ready?

ANATOL. In a moment. [*To the* WAITER] Did you understand? [WAITER *goes out.* ANATOL *comes down.*]

MAX. And suppose she doesn't come at all?

ANATOL. Why "at all?" It's just ten o'clock—she can't possibly be here before this.

MAX. The ballet was over some time ago.

ANATOL. Well? She has to get her make-up off, and change her clothes—I'd better run across and wait for her.

MAX. Don't spoil her.

ANATOL. Spoil her? If you knew—

MAX. Yes, yes, I know. You treat her brutally—but that's one way to spoil her.

ANATOL. That wasn't what I was going to say. If you only knew—

MAX. Well, say it—

ANATOL. I feel very solemn to-night.

MAX. You're not going to—to become engaged to her?

ANATOL. Oh, no, it's much more solemn.

MAX. You're going to marry her?

ANATOL. Oh, dear—how superficial you are. As if there was not a solemnity of the soul which has nothing whatever to do with all this external nonsense.

MAX. I see. Then you've discovered a hitherto unknown corner in the world of your emotions? And you think she understands?

ANATOL. You're very clumsy at guessing to-day. I am celebrating—the end.

MAX. Oh!

29

ANATOL. This is a farewell supper.

MAX. And what do you want me here for?

ANATOL. You are to close the eyes of our dead love.

MAX. Your comparison is in very bad taste.

ANATOL. I've been postponing this supper for a week.

MAX. You must have quite an appetite by this time.

ANATOL. Oh, we've been having supper together every evening all this week—but I couldn't find the right word—I didn't dare—you don't know how nervous it makes me.

MAX. And what do you need me for? You want me to give you the word?

ANATOL. It's just as well to have you here—in any case—I want you to assist me if it should be necessary. You can soften things—soothe her—make her understand—

MAX. Well, please tell me first why all this is necessary?

ANATOL. With pleasure—she bores me.

MAX. And you find someone else more amusing?

ANATOL. Yes—

MAX. I see.

ANATOL. Ah, the other—the other—

MAX. What type?

ANATOL. None at all—something quite new—something quite unique.

MAX. Yes, that's so—we never recognize the type until the last.

ANATOL. Imagine a girl—how shall I explain her—three-quarter rhythm.

MAX. You seem to be still under the influence of the ballet.

ANATOL. Yes—I can't help it—she reminds me of a slow Viennese waltz—sentimental cheeriness—smiling roguish melancholy,—that's what she is like—a sweet little blonde head, oh, it's too hard to describe—I feel so warm and content with her—when I give her a bunch of violets she receives it with a tear in the corner of her eye—

MAX. Try her with a bracelet some time.

ANATOL. Oh, dear man—that wouldn't do at all in this case—you're quite mistaken. And believe me, I wouldn't want to bring her here for supper. Her style is the cozy little cheap restaurant across the Line—with the hideous wall-paper and the petty official at the next table. That's the sort of place where I've been spending the last evenings, with her.

MAX. How's that? Didn't you just tell me that you'd been here with Annie?

ANATOL. Yes, that, too. I've eaten two suppers every evening last week—one with the girl I'm trying to win— the other with the girl I'm trying to lose. And I haven't been successful in either case.

MAX. I have a suggestion. Suppose you take Annie to a cheap restaurant and bring the new blonde here to supper —maybe that'll help.

ANATOL. Your comprehension of the situation is hampered by the fact that you don't know the new girl. She's the most modest creature in the world—why, you ought to see her, if I suggest ordering an expensive wine.

MAX. Tears in the corner of her eye?

ANATOL. She won't hear to it, under any condition.

MAX. Then you've been drinking Markersdorfer lately?

ANATOL. Yes—before ten o'clock—the champagne comes later. Such is life.

MAX. Oh, no—not always.

ANATOL. Imagine the contrast. But I've had enough of it. This is one of those cases where I feel that I am really a very honest nature—

MAX. Are you?

ANATOL. I can't stand this double game—I'm losing all my self-respect—

MAX. Oh, see here—it's only me—you needn't put on any airs with me.

ANATOL. Why not—seeing as you *are* here? But in all seriousness, I can't pretend to love where I don't feel anything more.

MAX. Then you only pretend where you do feel something—

ANATOL. I spoke to Annie honestly—in the very beginning—when we had exchanged our vows of eternal love—"Annie, dear," I said, "if either of us should feel, one fine day, that it's all over with our love, then we must confess it openly—"

MAX. You arranged all that just as you were vowing eternal love? That's very good.

ANATOL. I've repeated it frequently—"we have no responsibility towards one another—we are free—we can part calmly when the time has come—but there must be no deception—I abhor that."

MAX. Then it ought to be easy, this evening.

ANATOL. Easy? Now that the time has come, I'm afraid to say it—it will hurt her—and I can't endure tears. I may even fall in love with her again if she cries—and then I'll be deceiving the other.

MAX. Oh, no. No deception—I abhor that—

ANATOL. It'll all be much easier if you are here. There is a breath of cold, wholesome cheeriness about you, that will stiffen the sentimentality of the parting. One cannot weep in your presence.

MAX. Well, I'm here—but that's about all that I can do for you. You certainly don't want me to encourage her to let you go—do you? I could never do that—you're such a dear fellow.

ANATOL. Oh, well, you might try—up to a certain point, anyway. You might tell her that she isn't losing very much in me.

MAX. Yes, I might do that.

ANATOL. Tell her that she can find a hundred others, better looking—richer—

MAX. Cleverer—

ANATOL. Oh, no—you needn't exaggerate. [*The* WAITER *opens the door and* ANNIE *comes, with a raincoat hastily thrown over her dress, a white boa around her neck, her conspicuously big hat is put on anyhow, and she carries a pair of yellow gloves.*]

ANNIE. Oh, good evening.

ANATOL. Good evening, Annie. Excuse me for not—

ANNIE. You're a nice person to depend on. [*Throws off her coat*] I stand there, looking around—not a soul in sight.

ANATOL. You hadn't far to come—

ANNIE. But you ought to keep your promise. Good evening, Max. [*To* ANATOL] You might have let them begin serving. [ANATOL *kisses her.*]

ANNIE. I'm hungry. [*The* WAITER *knocks.*] Come in. He knocks today—it never occurred to him before. [*The* WAITER *comes in.*]

ANATOL. You can serve the supper. [*The* WAITER *goes out.*]

ANNIE. Were you in the opera house tonight?

ANATOL. No—I was obliged—

ANNIE. You didn't lose much—everybody was sleepy tonight—

MAX. What was the opera?

ANNIE. I don't know. [*They sit down at the table.*] I go to my dressing room—and then on to the stage—I never bother about the rest of it—by the way, I have something to tell you, Anatol.

ANATOL. Have you, dear? Anything important?

ANNIE. Yes, rather—it may surprise you. [*The* WAITER *comes in with dishes.*]

ANATOL. You make me curious. I, too—

ANNIE. Wait a moment— there's no necessity for him to hear it—

ANATOL [*to* WAITER]. You may go—we'll ring. [WAITER *goes out*.] Well?

ANNIE. Yes, my dear Anatol—it'll surprise you and yet I don't know—it shouldn't—no, it really shouldn't surprise you.

MAX. Have they raised your salary?

ANATOL. Don't interrupt her.

ANNIE. Why, you see, Anatol—say, are these Ostend or Whitstable?

ANATOL. Now she's talking about the oysters. They're Ostend.

ANNIE. I thought so—I do love oysters. It's really the only food that one can eat every day.

MAX. Not only can—but ought to.

ANNIE. Don't you think so?

ANATOL. But you had something important to tell me.

ANNIE. Yes—it is important—decidedly so. You remember a certain remark of yours?

ANATOL. Which? How can I possibly know which remark you mean?

MAX. No, he can't.

ANNIE. Why, I mean the—now wait a minute—how was it exactly? "Annie," you said, "we must never deceive one another—"

ANATOL. Yes, yes—well—

ANNIE. "Never deceive each other—it would be better to tell the entire truth."

ANATOL. Yes—I meant—

ANNIE. But if it's too late—

ANATOL. What's that?

ANNIE. No—it's not too late. I'm telling you in time—but only just in time. It may be too late to-morrow.

ANATOL. Are you crazy, Annie?

Max. How's that?

Annie. Anatol, you must eat your oysters—or I won't say another word.

Anatol. What does this mean? You must—

Annie. Eat!

Anatol. You must talk—I can't stand this sort of joke.

Annie. Well—didn't we arrange that we were to tell each other quite calmly—when the time came? The time has come.

Anatol. What time? What does this mean?

Annie. It means that this is my last supper with you.

Anatol. Will you have the kindness—to explain yourself?

Annie. It's all up between us.

Anatol. Yes—but—

Max. Oh, this is excellent—

Annie. What's so excellent about it? Well, I don't care —it's true.

Anatol. My dear girl—I still don't understand—have you had an offer of marriage?

Annie. Oh, if that was all—that would be no reason for getting rid of you.

Anatol. Getting rid of me?

Annie. I'll have to tell you—I am in love, Anatol—madly in love.

Anatol. And may I ask with whom?

Annie. Say, Max, what are you laughing at?

Max. This is very funny.

Anatol. Don't mind him. This is a matter between us two, Annie. You certainly owe me an explanation.

Annie. Well, I'm giving it to you. I have fallen in love with someone else. And I'm telling you openly—because that's the way it was arranged between us.

Anatol. Yes, but—who the devil—

Annie. My dear boy, you mustn't be coarse.

Anatol. I demand—I demand definitely—

ANNIE. Max, won't you please ring the bell. I'm so hungry.

ANATOL. Ha! She's hungry—hungry! At such a moment!

MAX. [to ANATOL]. Remember this is her *first* supper tonight. [*The* WAITER *comes in.*]

ANATOL. What do you want?

WAITER. You rang, sir.

MAX. Bring the next course. [WAITER *clears table.*]

ANNIE. Yes—Catalini's going to Germany, that's settled.

MAX. Indeed! And they're letting her go—without any fuss.

ANNIE. I don't know about that.

ANATOL [*pacing the room*]. The wine—where's the wine? Jean! Are you asleep?

WAITER. Here's the wine, sir.

ANATOL. I don't mean that wine—I mean the champagne—you know I want it with the first course. [WAITER *goes out.*] And now your explanation, please.

ANNIE. It's no use believing a word you men say—not a word. It sounded so nice when you said it, "When we feel that the end has come, we'll say so openly and we'll part peacefully."

ANATOL. Will you please finally—

ANNIE. This is what he calls being peaceful.

ANATOL. My dear girl—you can understand that it interests me, can't you? Who—

ANNIE. [*sipping the wine slowly*]. Ah—um—

ANATOL. Well, drink it.

ANNIE. You can wait a minute, can't you?

ANATOL. You generally drink it in one gulp—

ANNIE. But my dear Anatol, I'm saying good-bye to this Bordeaux. Goodness knows for how long.

ANATOL. What nonsense is this?

ANNIE. There'll be no Bordeaux for me—and no oysters —and no champagne—[*The* WAITER *comes with another dish, she looks at it.*]—and no Filet aux Truffes—that's all over.

MAX. What a sentimental appetite you have. May I give you some of this?

ANNIE. Thanks. [ANATOL *lights a cigarette.*]

MAX. Aren't you eating anything?

ANATOL. Not yet. [WAITER *goes out.*] And now I would really like to know—who the happy man is.

ANNIE. Suppose I should tell you his name,—you wouldn't know any more then.

ANATOL. What sort of a man is he? How did you come to know him? What does he look like?

ANNIE. Beautiful—he's beautiful! But that's all.

ANATOL. It seems to be enough for you.

ANNIE. Yes, there'll be no oysters now.

ANATOL. So you said.

ANNIE. And no champagne.

ANATOL. Confound it—he must have some other characteristic than the mere fact that he can't buy oysters and champagne for you.

MAX. He's right—that isn't what you might call a profession or an occupation.

ANNIE. But what does it matter—if I love him? I'm giving it all up—it's something quite new—something I've never experienced before.

MAX. Oh, but see here, Annie, if that's all it is, Anatol could have offered you a cheap supper, too.

ANATOL. What is he? A clerk? A chimney-sweep? A traveling salesman?

ANNIE. See here—you mustn't insult him—

MAX. Then why don't you tell us what he is?

ANNIE. He's an artist.

ANATOL. What kind of an artist—trapeze? That'll be something to your taste. A circus-rider?

ANNIE. Stop scolding. He's a colleague of mine.

ANATOL. Ah ha—an old acquaintance, eh? You've seen him daily for some years?—and you've been untrue to me for some time?

ANNIE. I shouldn't have said anything to you in that case. I depended on your word—that's why I'm confessing it to you before it's too late.

ANATOL. But you've been in love with him—Lord knows how long—you've been deceiving me—in spirit anyway.

ANNIE. Well, I can't help that.

ANATOL. You are a—

MAX. Anatol!

ANATOL. Do I know him?

ANNIE. I don't suppose you've noticed him—he dances in the chorus—but he'll be promoted—he'll be promoted.

ANATOL. And since when—have you discovered your heart?

ANNIE. Since this evening.

ANATOL. Don't lie to me.

ANNIE. I'm telling you the truth. This evening—I knew it was my Fate.

ANATOL. Her fate—do you hear that, Max? Her fate.

ANNIE. Well, a thing like that is fate.

ANATOL. But I want to know all about it—I have a right to know—you're still mine in this moment—I want to know how long this has been going on—I want to know when it began—I want to know how he dared—

MAX. Yes, you really ought to tell us.

ANNIE. This is what I get for being so honest—um—I ought to have done the way Fritzi did—with her Baron. He don't know anything yet, and she's been running around for three months with a Hussar Lieutenant.

ANATOL. The Baron will find it out some of these days.

ANNIE. Maybe—but you'd never have found it out—never—I'm much too slick for that—and you're much too stupid. [*Pours out a glass of wine*].

ANATOL. Stop drinking.

ANNIE. Not much. I want to get a jag tonight—it'll probably be the last.

MAX. For a week?

ANNIE. Forever. I'll stay with Carl because I'm really fond of him—and he's so jolly even if he hasn't any money and he don't make me angry—and he's a dear, dear, sweet boy.

ANATOL. You haven't kept your promise—you've been in love with him ever so long—that's a stupid lie—that talk about this evening.

ANNIE. You needn't believe it if you don't want to.

MAX. Now, Annie, do tell the story straight—or not at all. If you want to part calmly, you ought to do this for him, for your Anatol—

ANATOL. Then I'll tell you something, too.

ANNIE. Well, it began—[*The* WAITER *comes in.*]

ANATOL. Go on. [*Sits down beside her.*]

ANNIE. It was about two weeks ago—or maybe a little longer—when he brought a couple of roses—at the stage door. It made me laugh—he looked so shy.

ANATOL. You didn't tell me that.

ANNIE. What was there to tell?

ANATOL. Well, go on.

ANNIE. And then at rehearsal—he hung around me—in such a funny way—and I noticed it. It made me mad at first—and then I was glad.

ANATOL. Quite simple, I see.

ANNIE. And then we began to talk to each other—and everything about him pleased me.

ANATOL. What did you talk about?

ANNIE. All sorts of things—he told me how they'd put

him out of school—and how he'd tried to learn a trade—and then the real stage blood in him began to make itself felt—

ANATOL. You've never told me any of that—

ANNIE. And then what do you think? Then it came out that when we were children we lived in the same street—just two houses apart.

ANATOL. Neighbors—how touching!

ANNIE. Yes, isn't it? [*Drinks.*]

ANATOL. Go on.

ANNIE. There's nothing more—I've told you everything. It's my Fate—and you can't do anything against Fate—no —you—can't—do anything—when it's Fate.

ANATOL. But I want to know about this evening.

ANNIE. What about—? [*Her head sinks back.*]

MAX. She's going to sleep.

ANATOL. Wake her up. Put the wine where she can't see it—I must know what happened this evening. Annie— Annie—

ANNIE. This evening—he told me—that he—loved me.

ANATOL. And you?

ANNIE. I told him—that I was very glad. And because I don't want to—to deceive him—I'll say good-bye to you.

ANATOL. Because you don't want to deceive *him*? Then it isn't for my sake—but for his?

ANNIE. What's the matter with you? I don't love you any more.

ANATOL. Ah ha—that was good! Fortunately I don't mind this now.

ANNIE. Indeed!

ANATOL. Because I, too, am in the same fortunate situa-tion—I can get along without your affection now.

ANNIE. Oh, can you?

ANATOL. I can. I haven't loved you for some time—I love someone else.

ANNIE. Ha! Ha!

ANATOL. Ask Max. I told him all about it before you came in.

ANNIE. Did you?

ANATOL. I haven't loved you for some time—the other is a thousand times better and more beautiful.

ANNIE. Indeed!

ANATOL. I'd give a thousand women like you for one such girl—do you hear? [ANNIE *laughs.*] You needn't laugh —ask Max.

ANNIE. This is awfully funny—you're trying to make me believe—

ANATOL. But it's true I tell you—I swear it's true. I haven't loved you for ever so long. I haven't thought of you—not even while I was here with you. And when I kissed you I was thinking of the other—the other—

ANNIE. Well—then we're quits.

ANATOL. Do you think so?

ANNIE. Yes, we're quits—and I'm glad of it.

ANATOL. No, we're not quits—not at all—it's not the same thing—your experience and mine. My story is not quite so—innocent.

ANNIE. [*more serious*]. What's that?

ANATOL. My story sounds somewhat different.

ANNIE. Why is it different?

ANATOL. Why, I—I have been untrue to you.

ANNIE [*rising*]. What?

ANATOL. I've deceived you—as you deserve. Day by day —night after night—I came from her when I met you—and returned to her when I left you.

ANNIE. That—is—infamous! [*She goes to hatstand, throws on her coat and boa.*]

ANATOL. One can't be quick enough with women like you —or else they'll get ahead of one—well, fortunately, I have no illusions.

ANNIE. Yes, there you can see—

ANATOL. Exactly.

ANNIE. You can see that a man is a hundred times less considerate than a woman.

ANATOL. Exactly. I'm not considerate—

ANNIE. [*winds her boa around her throat, takes up her gloves, stands in front of* ANATOL]. No, you're certainly not! I wouldn't have told you—*that*. [*She turns to go.*]

ANATOL. What's that?

MAX. Let her go. You don't want to stop her, do you?

ANATOL. You wouldn't have told me—*that?* You mean that you—that you—

ANNIE [*at the door*]. I *never* would have told you— never—never—it takes a man to be so inconsiderate! [*The* WAITER *comes in with a dish of dessert.*]

ANATOL. Take that stuff away.

ANNIE. What's that? [*Looks at it*] Vanilla cream? Oh!

ANATOL. You dare?

MAX. Oh, let her—she has to say good-bye to the cream —forever.

ANNIE. Yes, and I'm glad to do it, too. And to say good-bye to the Bordeaux and the champagne—and the oysters —but most particularly am I glad to say good-bye to you, Anatol. [*Suddenly, with a vulgar laugh, she pounces on the box of cigarettes on a side table and takes out a handful, putting them in her bag.*]

ANNIE. These aren't for me—I'm taking them for him. [*Goes out.* ANATOL *moves as if to follow, then stops by the door.*]

MAX [*calmly*]. There, you see—it was very easy after all.

CURTAIN

THE LOST SILK HAT

BY

LORD DUNSANY

From *Five Plays* by Lord Dunsany, Copyright, 1914, by Little, Brown and Company.

PERSONS

THE CALLER
THE LABORER
THE CLERK
THE POET
THE POLICEMAN

SCENE: *A fashionable London street.*

THE CALLER *stands on a doorstep, "faultlessly dressed,"*
but without a hat. At first he shows despair, then a new
thought engrosses him.

Enter THE LABORER.

THE CALLER. Excuse me a moment. Excuse me—but—
I'd be greatly obliged to you if—if you could see your way
—in fact, you can be of great service to me if—

THE LABORER. Glad to do what I can, sir.

CALLER. Well, all I really want you to do is just to ring
that bell and go up and say—er—say that you've come to
see to the drains, or anything like that, you know, and
get hold of my hat for me.

LABORER. Get hold of your 'at!

CALLER. Yes. You see, I left my hat behind most unfortunately. It's in the drawing room [*points to window*],
that room there, half under the long sofa, the far end from
the door. And if you could possibly go and get it, why I'd
be [*The* LABORER'S *expression changes.*]—Why, what's
the matter?

LABORER [*firmly*]. I don't like this job.

CALLER. Don't like this job! But my dear fellow, don't
be silly, what possible harm—?

LABORER. Ah-h. That's what I don't know.

44

CALLER. But what harm can there possibly be in so simple a request? What harm does there seem to be?

LABORER. Oh, it seems all right.

CALLER. *Well*, then.

LABORER. All these crack jobs do seem all right.

CALLER. But I'm not asking you to rob the house.

LABORER. Don't seem as if you are, certainly, but I don't like the looks of it; what if there's things what I can't 'elp taking when I gets inside?

CALLER. I only want my hat— Here, I say, please don't go away—here's a sovereign, it will only take you a minute.

LABORER. *What I want to know—*

CALLER. Yes?

LABORER. What's *in* that hat?

CALLER. What's *in* the hat?

LABORER. Yes; that's what I want to know.

CALLER. What's in the hat?

LABORER. Yes, you aren't going to give me a sovereign—?

CALLER. I'll give you two sovereigns.

LABORER. You aren't going to give me a sovereign, and rise it to two sovereigns, for an *empty* hat?

CALLER. But I must have my hat. I can't be seen in the streets like this. There's nothing *in* the hat. What do you think's in the hat?

LABORER. Ah, I'm not clever enough to say that, but it looks as if the papers was in that hat.

CALLER. The papers?

LABORER. Yes, papers proving, if you can get them, that you're the heir to that big house, and some poor innocent will be defrauded.

CALLER. Look here, the hat's absolutely empty. I *must* have my hat. If there's anything in it you shall have it yourself as well as the two pounds, only get me my hat.

LABORER. Well, that seems all right.

CALLER. That's right, then you'll run up and get it?

LABORER. Seems all right to me and seems all right to you. But it's the police what you and I have got to think of. Will it seem all right to them?

CALLER. Oh, for heaven's sake—

LABORER. Ah!

CALLER. What a hopeless fool you are.

LABORER. Ah!

CALLER. Look here.

LABORER. Ah, I got you there, mister.

CALLER. Look here, for goodness sake don't go.

LABORER. Ah! [*Exit*]

[*Enter* THE CLERK.]

CALLER. Excuse me, sir. Excuse my asking you, but, as you see, I am without a hat. I shall be extraordinarily obliged to you if you would be so very good as to get it for me. Pretend you have come to wind the clocks, you know. I left it in the drawing-room of this house, half under the long sofa, the far end.

CLERK. Oh, er—all right, only—

CALLER. Thanks so much, I am immensely indebted to you. Just say you've come to wind the clocks, you know.

CLERK. I—er—don't think I'm very good at winding clocks, you know.

CALLER. Oh, that's all right, just stand in front of the clock and fool about with it. That's all they ever do. I must warn you there's a lady in the room.

CLERK. Oh!

CALLER. But that's all right, you know. Just walk past up to the clock.

CLERK. But I think, if you don't mind, as there's some-one there—

CALLER. Oh, but she's quite young and very, very beautiful and—

CLERK. Why don't you get it yourself?

CALLER. That is impossible.

CLERK. Impossible?

CALLER. Yes, I have sprained my ankle.

CLERK. Oh! Is it bad?

CALLER. Yes, very bad indeed.

CLERK. I don't mind trying to carry you up.

CALLER. No, that would be worse. My foot has to be kept on the ground.

CLERK. But how will you get home?

CALLER. I can walk all right on the flat.

CLERK. I'm afraid I have to be going on. It's rather later than I thought.

CALLER. But for goodness sake don't leave me. You can't leave me here like this without a hat.

CLERK. I'm afraid I must, it's later than I thought. [*Exit*]
[*Enter* THE POET.]

CALLER. Excuse me, sir. Excuse my stopping you. But I should be immensely obliged to you if you would do me a very great favor. I have unfortunately left my hat behind while calling at this house. It is half under the long sofa, at the far end. If you could possibly be so kind as to pretend you have come to tune the piano and fetch my hat for me I should be enormously grateful to you.

POET. But why cannot you get it for yourself?

CALLER. I cannot.

POET. If you would tell me the reason perhaps I could help you.

CALLER. I cannot. I can never enter that house again.

POET. If you have committed a murder, by all means tell me. I am not sufficiently interested in ethics to wish to have you hanged for it.

CALLER. Do I look like a murderer?

POET. No, of course not. I am only saying that you can safely trust me, for not only does the statute book and its penalties rather tend to bore me, but murder itself has always had a certain fascination for me. I write delicate and fastidious lyrics, yet, strange as it may appear, I read every murder trial, and my sympathies are always with the prisoner.

CALLER. But I tell you I am not a murderer.

POET. Then what have you done?

CALLER. I have quarrelled with a lady in that house and have sworn to join the Bosnians and die in Africa.

POET. But this is beautiful.

CALLER. Unfortunately I forgot my hat.

POET. You go to die for a hopeless love, and in a far country; it was the wont of the troubadours.

CALLER. But you will get my hat for me?

POET. That I will gladly do for you. But we must find an adequate reason for entering the house.

CALLER. You pretend to tune the piano.

POET. That, unfortunately, is impossible. The sound of a piano being unskilfully handled is to me what the continual drop of cold water on the same part of the head is said to be in countries where that interesting torture is practised. There is—

CALLER. But what are we to do?

POET. There is a house where kind friends of mine have given me that security and comfort that are a poet's necessity. But there was a governess there and a piano. It is years and years since I was able even to see the faces of those friends without an inward shudder.

CALLER. Well, we'll have to think of something else.

POET. You are bringing back to these unhappy days the romance of an age of which the ballads tell us that kings sometimes fought in no other armor than their lady's nightshirt.

CALLER. Yes, but you know first of all I must get my hat.

POET. But why?

CALLER. I cannot possibly be seen in the streets without a hat.

POET. Why not?

CALLER. It can't be done.

POET. But you confuse externals with essentials.

CALLER. I don't know what you call essentials, but being decently dressed in London seems pretty essential to me.

POET. A hat is not one of the essential things of life.

CALLER. I don't want to appear rude, but my hat isn't quite like yours.

POET. Let us sit down and talk of things that matter, things that will be remembered after a hundred years. [*They sit.*] Regarded in this light one sees at once the triviality of hats. But to die, and die beautifully for a hopeless love, that is a thing one could make a lyric about. That is the test of essential things—try and imagine them in a lyric. One could not write a lyric about a hat.

CALLER. I don't care whether you could write a lyric about my hat or whether you couldn't. All I know is that I am not going to make myself absolutely ridiculous by walking about in London without a hat. Will you get it for me or will you not?

POET. To take any part in the tuning of a piano is impossible to me.

CALLER. Well, pretend you've come to look at the radiator. They have one under the window, and I happen to know it leaks.

POET. I suppose it has an artistic decoration on it.

CALLER. Yes, I think so.

POET. Then I decline to look at it or to go near it. I know these decorations in cast iron. I once saw a pot-bellied Egyptian god, named Bĕs, and he was *meant* to be ugly, but he wasn't as ugly as these decorations that the twentieth century can make with machinery. What has a plumber got to do with art that he should dare to attempt decoration?

CALLER. Then you won't help me.

POET. I won't look at ugly things and I won't listen to ugly noises, but if you can think of any reasonable plan I don't mind helping you.

CALLER. I can think of nothing else. You don't look like a plumber or a clock-winder. I can think of nothing more. I have had a terrible ordeal and I am not in the condition to think calmly.

POET. Then you will have to leave your hat to its altered destiny.

CALLER. Why can't you think of a plan? If you're a poet, thinking's rather in your line.

POET. If I could bring my thoughts to contemplate so absurd a thing as a hat for any length of time no doubt I could think of a plan, but the very triviality of the theme seems to scare them away.

CALLER [rising]. Then I must get it myself.

POET. For Heaven's sake, don't do that! Think what it means!

CALLER. I know it will seem absurd, but not so absurd as walking through London without it.

POET. I don't mean that. But you will make it up. You will forgive each other, and you will marry her and have a family of noisy, pimply children like everyone else, and Romance will be dead. No, don't ring that bell. Go and buy a bayonet, or whatever one does buy, and join the Bosnians.

CALLER. I tell you I can't without a hat.

POET. What is a hat! Will you sacrifice for it a beautiful doom? Think of your bones, neglected and forgotten, lying forlornly because of hopeless love on endless golden sands. "Lying forlorn!" as Keats said. What a word! Forlorn in Africa. The careless Bedouins going past by day, at night the lion's roar, the grievous voice of the desert.

CALLER. As a matter of fact, I don't think you're right in speaking of it as desert. The Bosnians, I believe, are only taking it because it is supposed to be the most fertile land in the world.

POET. What of that? You will not be remembered by geography and statistics, but by golden-mouthed Romance. And that is how Romance sees Africa.

CALLER. Well, I'm going to get my hat.

POET. Think! Think! If you enter by that door you will never fall among the foremost Bosnians. You will never die in a far-off, lonely land to lie by immense Sahara. And she will never weep for your beautiful doom and call herself cruel in vain.

CALLER. Hark! She is playing the piano. It seems to me that she might be unhappy about it for years. I don't see much good in that.

POET. No. *I* will comfort her.

CALLER. I'm damned if you do! Look here! I don't mind saying, I'm damned if you do.

POET. Calm yourself. Calm yourself. I do not mean in that way.

CALLER. Then what on earth do you mean?

POET. I will make songs about your beautiful death, glad songs and sad songs. They shall be glad because they tell again the noble tradition of the troubadours, and sad because they tell of your sorrowful destiny and of your hopeless love.

I shall make legends also about your lonely bones, telling perhaps how some Arabian men, finding them in the desert by some oasis, memorable in war, wonder who loved them. And then as I read them to her, she weeps perhaps a little, and I read instead of the glory of the soldier, how it overtops our transitory—

CALLER. Look here, I'm not aware that you've ever been introduced to her.

POET. A trifle, a trifle.

CALLER. It seems to me that you're in rather an undue hurry for me to get a Jubu spear in me; but I'm going to get my hat first.

POET. I appeal to you. I appeal to you in the name of beautiful battles, high deeds, and lost causes; in the name of love-tales told to cruel maidens and told in vain. In the name of stricken hearts broken like beautiful harp-strings, I appeal to you. I appeal in the ancient holy name of Romance: *do not ring that bell.* [CALLER *rings the bell.*]

POET. [*sits down, abject*]. You will marry. You will sometimes take a ticket with your wife as far as Paris. Perhaps as far as Cannes. Then the family will come; a large sprawling family as far as the eye can see (I speak in hyperbole). You'll earn money and feed it and be like all the rest. No monument will ever be set up to your memory but —[*Servant answers bell.* CALLER *says something inaudible. Exit through door.*]

POET. [*rising, lifting hand*]. But let there be graven in brass upon this house: Romance was born again here out of due time and died young. [*He sits down. Enter* LABORER *and* CLERK *with* POLICEMAN. *The music stops.*]

POET. Everything's wrong. They're going to kill Romance.

POLICEMAN [*to* LABORER] This gentleman doesn't seem quite right somehow.

LABORER. They're none of them quite right to-day.

[*Music starts again.*]

POET. My God! It is a duet.

POLICEMAN. He seems a bit wrong somehow.

LABORER. You should 'a seen the other one.

CURTAIN

THE SISTERS' TRAGEDY

BY

RICHARD HUGHES

From *Richard Hughes—An Omnibus*: Harper and Brothers, Publishers. Application for amateur performance of this play should be addressed to Baker International Play Bureau, 41 Winter Street, Boston. Application for professional and other rights should be addressed to the Author, c/o Harper & Brothers.

CHARACTERS

They are all rather slovenly in appearance, suggesting a family possibly of county origin but for at least a generation impoverished and isolated and uneducated.

PHILIPPA is about twenty-eight, plain, with a rather grim mouth. She is elaborately but untidily and unfashionably dressed, in a way out of keeping with a country life.

OWEN is about twenty-four, tall and very thin, with the vacant, peevish air of a blind deaf-mute. The only sound he makes is a sort of throaty chuckle (referred to as "Owen's noise") by which he attracts attention to his wants, which he explains in dumbshow. His jaw drops rather.

CHARLOTTE is nineteen: a pretty, fair (but rather hard and characterless) face: she would look very pretty if properly dressed and taught how to walk and hold herself. When she enters, she is wearing an old pair of army riding-breeches and a torn silk evening jumper: her hair wildish.

LOWRIE is about thirteen, and very small and slight. She is superficially like CHARLOTTE, but not so pretty, and far more passionate and sensitive. All are bitten with the prevalent Welsh piety of the neighborhood; but in LOWRIE only does her imaginative power and curious trend of logic render this dangerous.

JOHN, who is by way of being CHARLOTTE's fiance, is quite obviously of a lower social class than the sisters, though they do not appear to see it; which completes the general air of running to seed. This vulgarity only becomes quite patent under the stress of emotion at the end of the play. In the first scene with LOWRIE his manner is a little bewildered, but good-natured; and he seems quite fond of her. One's

first impression from their manner is that he is more in love
with CHARLOTTE than she with him.

SCENE—*The hall in the sisters' house (an early-Victorian
mansion in the Welsh hills), now used as a living-room.
There is a front door up R., with a window to the left of it;
a fire L., with an arm-chair facing the audience and another below it; and a door above it; a table littered with
work-things, etc., centre. The walls are panelled, and there
are dingy oil portraits, some of them torn; mostly crooked.
The fur hearth-rug is moulted: a general air of past pros-
perity run to seed, untidiness, things put to their wrong
uses. Decoration, such as it is, Victorian.*

TIME—*Autumn, early afternoon.*

PHILIPPA *discovered at window, looking out, one arm in
a half-darned stocking.*

PHILIPPA. Kill it, Chattie, kill it!
CHARLOTTE [*without; exasperated*]. I can't.
PHILIPPA. Put it out of its pain at once, for heaven's
sake.
CHARLOTTE [*without*]. I can't do it: you come.
PHILIPPA. Pull yourself together, Charlotte; hit it be-
hind the ears with your shoe. Oh, be quick, it's screaming.
[*Sound of a blow; steps heard running.*]
LOWRIE [*off*]. Oh, you brute, Chattie, what are you do-
ing?
CHARLOTTE [*off*]. I've missed it.
LOWRIE [*off*]. Stop! Stop! It might live! [*Another
blow.*] O—oh, beast!
CHARLOTTE [*off*]. It's dead now, poor little thing. [*Enter
CHARLOTTE by door up, dressed as above, hot but pale. She
fits her shoe on in the doorway.*] It's dead now. It's a

beastly business. I wish I hadn't been there and had to do it, it would have died anyhow in time. Somehow I couldn't hit straight, like in a dream. Silly of me. Cats are brutes.

PHILIPPA [*sitting down*]. I thought you were never going to finish.

CHARLOTTE. It must have been the little Joneses' rabbit got loose; Ginger could never have caught a wild one. I wish they'd look after it better, instead of letting it run about the garden and treating it like a pet. Poor little Anne, though.

PHILIPPA. It will be a lesson to her not to get so fond of brute animals. It isn't right.

CHARLOTTE. Well, *you* can tell her so. I've had enough of the whole business: she'll cry.—Lowrie has gone silly over it too: look at her. [*Enter* LOWRIE *by door up, with something in her arms. Her head is bent forward, so that her long, loose hair covers her face. She moves quickly.*]

PHILIPPA. Don't bring it in the house, Lowrie. It must be buried.

LOWRIE [*to* PHILIPPA]. You brute, you told her to do it! Look at the blood in its eyes! [*To* CHARLOTTE:] Oh, you beast, Chattie, you murderer! You brute, though you are my sister, you— [*She bursts into tears and rushes as if to hit her.*]

PHILIPPA [*in a harsh voice*]. Lowrie. [LOWRIE *stops dead.*]

PHILIPPA. Put that rabbit down! [LOWRIE *does so.*] You dare hit your sister. What do you mean by behaving like this!

LOWRIE. She killed it.

PHILIPPA. She killed it to put it out of pain.

LOWRIE. Killing's murder.

PHILIPPA. You little fool, would you have let it go on screaming in agony?

LOWRIE. We might have nursed it.

CHARLOTTE [*huffily*]. Its back was broken.

LOWRIE. Do you mean it can ever be right to kill?

PHILIPPA. Of course it's right to put a thing out of its pain, you little idiot, when living is only a burden to it.

LOWRIE [*nervously*]. I don't know. Perhaps I'm silly. I thought there wasn't any arguing about killing: I thought it was just *wrong*. But are you sure it's right?—The Commandments, I mean . . .

PHILIPPA. Of course it's right, when it's done from high motives. You don't think John was wrong to shoot Germans, do you?

LOWRIE. No, of course, but Germans are different: this was a rabbit. Besides, it was his duty to do it.

CHARLOTTE. Well, you don't think I killed the little thing for pleasure, do you? Did I look as if I enjoyed it? I wish you'd be a bit more considerate of my feelings: I didn't want to do it, and then you make it all the worse for me by going on like this.

LOWRIE [*turning to her, with change of expression*]. Oh, Chattie, I'm so sorry, I'm a beast. I didn't think. Do forgive me. I didn't see it like that, and I've been a brute to you. I must think about it all.

PHILIPPA. Very well, then; now you've said you're sorry for your selfishness, you had better go away to your room till you feel better.

[*Exit* LOWRIE. CHARLOTTE *picks up the rabbit carelessly and strokes its fur; she sits down.*]

CHARLOTTE. Thank goodness that's over.

PHILIPPA. I don't think we shall have any more trouble from her. She has these naughty tempers, but once she has said she's sorry, she calms down.

CHARLOTTE. She's got a logical sort of mind, you know: once she sees a point, like that, she goes on ruminating on it for days.

PHILIPPA. She has no need to! She has far too many ideas of her own about right and wrong for her age, that child.

She ought to be content to do what she's told, instead of always reasoning about it.

CHARLOTTE. Oh, well, I think we're through with this storm.

PHILIPPA. I'm not sure. You can never be quite sure with her. But I expect we are. It's a pity she was by; but she has got to meet that sort of thing some time.

CHARLOTTE. Shall we get John to skin it? If he killed another too, it would make a pair of slippers.

PHILIPPA. Oh, Charlotte, *could* you!

CHARLOTTE. Why not? You're as bad as Lowrie.

PHILIPPA. It doesn't seem right to make any *use* of a thing you have killed.

CHARLOTTE. I don't see it.

PHILIPPA. Well, let's talk about something more cheerful.

CHARLOTTE. What?

PHILIPPA. John.

CHARLOTTE [*in a lustreless voice*]. If you like.

PHILIPPA. When are you going to marry him?

CHARLOTTE. I don't know. Never.

PHILIPPA. You're a goose.

CHARLOTTE [*exasperated*]. Phil, how can I? How am I ever going to get away from this place?

PHILIPPA [*coldly*]. I say you are a goose. I am enough to look after Owen.

CHARLOTTE. How could I marry John and leave you to look after him all your life? People would jolly soon make my life a misery for me, for neglecting my duty. I know them!

PHILIPPA. Nonsense! You could go and live somewhere else.

CHARLOTTE. And what about you, anyway? Why should your life be sacrificed to him?

PHILIPPA. It's the Lord's will.

CHARLOTTE. You haven't spent a night away from the house for three years.

PHILIPPA. Why should I? I've got used to it. I—I should feel funny without dear old Owen. Anyhow, *I* don't want to get married.

CHARLOTTE. Have you never wanted to?

PHILIPPA [*pause*]. No [*meaning* "yes"].

CHARLOTTE. I suppose it's all right for you, then, if you're built that way. Self-sacrifice, I mean. But I'm not. I intend to get away some time.

PHILIPPA. Then go at once! Why not?

CHARLOTTE [*fiercely*]. Haven't I already told you I can't?

PHILIPPA. Don't worry about me! I am only doing what is right. I shall never regret it; not in this world, and I shall have my reward in the next. I intend to devote my whole life to Owen, and so make an offering acceptable unto the Lord.

CHARLOTTE. I see: you would prefer to be martyred comfortably at home, than have it done in some unhealthy jungle. It's not a bad idea.

PHILIPPA. Chattie! How can you! You forget one must not think of oneself in these matters, but of the object. It is Owen I am thinking of; my duty lies at home; surely I may thank God for that small mercy without thereby forfeiting the full reward? It is wicked of you to put it like that, it's unkind, when all I am trying to do is to free you from your duty.

CHARLOTTE. It's not my duty you're trying to free me from, it's my conscience.

PHILIPPA. Is it your conscience is troubling you? Or what people will say, and perhaps the heavenly consequences?

CHARLOTTE. Oh, shut up, Phil, you beast! Aren't I refusing to go? What more do you want? Besides, Owen may be taken away, and then I *can* marry, and your old conscience can take you to Somaliland or anywhere else horrid.

PHILIPPA. If you *like* to keep John waiting till you're sixty, of course—

[*Enter* LOWRIE *by door L. The sisters do not notice her, but she must never let the audience forget her presence during the scene, to which she pays a sort of abstracted attention. She picks up a book, but does not read it attentively.*]

CHARLOTTE [*suddenly*]. Phil, it's a shame! I almost *hate* Owen when I see how he is wearing you out.

PHILIPPA. You mustn't talk like that, Chattie; you don't know how you hurt me. You never knew Owen like I did, before it happened. He was only seven. I shall always love him.

CHARLOTTE. All the same, it's a shame about all of us. Why should you and I and John have our lives spoilt for the sake of Owen, whose life really isn't worth living? Besides, it must be almost more awful for him than if he had been *born* blind and deaf, to lose them like that suddenly when he was seven years old, just through catching measles, and then to forget, actually to *forget* how to speak, too!— Phil, it makes me go cold to say it, but can God be just and merciful when he does things like that?

PHILIPPA. We are told that suffering is sent to chasten us.

CHARLOTTE. Told! Oh, yes, we're *told* often enough.

PHILIPPA. Oh, do stop! You're making it harder for me to bear, and God knows it is hard enough already. But there's no need if that's how you feel: haven't I always told you you are free to go away at any time? You won't do any good to yourself or anyone else by staying on in that frame of mind.

CHARLOTTE. And you?

PHILIPPA. I can bear it. It is what I am *for*.

CHARLOTTE. I can't go! I know you'll say it's wicked,

but I almost pray that Owen may die. What's life to him, anyway? He isn't really alive, and he's killing you. Surely even in God's eyes your life is worth more than his.

PHILIPPA. Don't talk like that.

CHARLOTTE. I can't help *thinking* like that.

PHILIPPA. It's wicked; what good does it do, anyhow? Who are you to try and alter God's will? Besides, He may already have decided to take Owen to Him in His own way, by His own instrument unknown and even unguessed at by us. We know that He has never forgotten. Promise me you won't pray it.

CHARLOTTE. I can't promise.

PHILIPPA. You must, or I'll be miserable.

CHARLOTTE. Very well, then: but I'll still *think* it.

PHILIPPA. Where is he now, do you know?

CHARLOTTE. No, but I suppose he will be along presently.

[LOWRIE *gets up, and walks down the stage, carrying the book.* PHILIPPA's *and* CHARLOTTE's *manner changes immediately.*]

PHILIPPA. Reading?

LOWRIE [*wandering about aimlessly*]. Mm.

PHILIPPA. What?

LOWRIE. A tale. It was very silly.

PHILIPPA. Why don't you read better books, then?

LOWRIE. Because I don't like better books. It was about Mr. Badger. It's a story, at any rate. Have animals got Christian souls?

PHILIPPA. Why?

LOWRIE. I wondered. About that rabbit too: would he go to heaven?

PHILIPPA. No, he wouldn't go anywhere: he'd just die. But being nothing would be better for him than lingering on.

LOWRIE. It's better for Christians to go to heaven, anyhow, isn't it? I mean, however happy they are here, they'll be happier there, won't they? When old Mrs. Rhys died of the rheumatics, you said it was a merciful release. You told Ellen what a beautiful place her Grannie had gone to, didn't you, Phil? It's never just dying into blackness for a Christian, is it?

PHILIPPA. What are you asking such questions for?

LOWRIE. Is everyone who was christened Christian?

PHILIPPA. Why, yes.

LOWRIE. You're quite sure about all this?

PHILIPPA [*sharply*]. Quite.

LOWRIE. I suppose you're right. You must be. [PHILIPPA *catches* CHARLOTTE's *eye.*]

CHARLOTTE. Lowrie, did you feed the bird to-day?

LOWRIE. No.

CHARLOTTE. Yesterday?

LOWRIE. I don't remember.

CHARLOTTE. Why can't you attend to your ordinary daily duties, instead of worrying about things like this which don't concern you? You'd better go and see whether *he's* alive still, instead of arguing about people dying. [*Exit* LOWRIE *by door L.*] What a little devil she is for questioning! What is she getting at?

PHILIPPA. I don't know: there's obviously something running in her head. The worst of her is that whenever she gets into her head that something is right, she does it. It wouldn't matter otherwise.

CHARLOTTE. Do you think *she's* going to pray for Owen to die?

PHILIPPA. I shouldn't think so; but you never can tell. I'll have to talk to her some time. Do you remember the time when she wouldn't eat meat, on her conscience? Why must she always be putting her twos to her twos, instead of leaving them quietly apart as the good God has put them? It's a bad habit, and makes me very worried about her sometimes.— Is John coming up to-day?

CHARLOTTE. I believe so: he's supposed to be going riding with me this afternoon. He ought to be here by now: I had forgotten.

PHILIPPA. *Forgotten!*

CHARLOTTE. Why not?

PHILIPPA. Oh—Aren't you going to change that jumper?

CHARLOTTE. No. Why should I?

PHILIPPA. John, I mean.

CHARLOTTE. Oh, he won't mind. [*Re-enter* LOWRIE.] Is he still alive?

LOWRIE. [*jumping*]. Who? Why?

CHARLOTTE. The bird.

LOWRIE. The bird? Oh, yes, I had fed him after all, and forgotten.

PHILIPPA. [*to* CHARLOTTE]. I'd change it if I were you.

CHARLOTTE. Why? What does it matter?

[*There is a sound of hoofs off, and a voice calling* "Chattie."]

PHILIPPA. Hallo! Come right in. [*Enter* JOHN.]

CHARLOTTE. All right, I'm coming.

PHILIPPA. [*aside*]. Well, at any rate let me sew it up.

[*Exeunt together* PHILIPPA *and* CHARLOTTE *L.*]

JOHN [*warming his hands*]. Well, Lowrie, how's life?

LOWRIE. If you were driving a trap, John, and the wheel rolled over something small in the road, and hurt it desperately but not so as quite to kill it, what would you do?

JOHN. I'm tender-hearted, kid; unless I was in a hurry I'd give it a belt with the whip-handle, or perhaps a stone, to put it out of its pain.

LOWRIE. You're sure that's right?

JOHN. Why, of course.

LOWRIE. And yet animals don't have an after-life, do they? It's really much more killing to kill an animal than to kill a person?

JOHN. What do you mean?

LOWRIE. I don't know.—John, are you going to marry Chattie?

JOHN [*sharply*]. Who said?

LOWRIE. But why shouldn't you?

JOHN [*slowly*]. I'm not saying I shouldn't.

LOWRIE. Then why don't you? Is it because of Owen?

JOHN. Why?

LOWRIE. I wish he was dead.

JOHN. You mustn't say that, Lowrie, it's wicked.

LOWRIE. Don't *you?*

JOHN. I wouldn't *say* so.

LOWRIE. I can't see the difference. It's no great joy to him being alive, and if he was dead he would be in heaven, and you and Chattie could get married. What's wrong in that? He'd have ears and eyes in heaven.

JOHN. I'm not saying it wouldn't be better for *him*.

LOWRIE. Who wouldn't it be better for, then? What's Owen *for?*

JOHN. Well, he makes Phil able to live a life of self-sacrifice, and that's the best life a Christian *can* lead.

LOWRIE. Self-sacrifice is what's right?

JOHN. Of course it is. It makes people holy.

LOWRIE. Then you mean that really he is being sacrificed to her, not her to him? It's all very muddly.

[OWEN's *noise heard off L., then fingers feeling on the door.* LOWRIE *runs to it, opens it, takes his arm, and leads him down to the chair by the fire facing the audience. This to be done slowly and emphatically. She comes back to* JOHN.]

LOWRIE [*to* JOHN]. Let him feel your sleeve [*does so*]. He likes to know who's here. Jack, you must make her marry you soon, and put Owen into a hospital somewhere. It's all very well to say suffering makes people holy: it isn't with her and Phil, it's making them ill-tempered; that's what it does with most people, it makes them cross and ill-tempered, and perhaps she won't go to heaven in the end at all, she's so snappy sometimes. Oh, John, I do love them. I'd do anything to make them happy, but I'll never be any use to anyone; but if only Owen would die, you could marry Chattie, and if Phil has a rest, she'd get quite young again.

[OWEN's *noise, and he puts two fingers to his lips, sucking.* LOWRIE *lights a cigarette and gives it to him.*]

LOWRIE. When I was older I would offer to look after Owen myself, because I really love him too, only I know Phil would never let me, so that would be no good. I'd give my life not to see Phil unhappy like this: I'd let God send my soul to hell for her sake; that's sacrifice, isn't it?

JOHN. Lowrie, you're blaspheming! You're a good girl, but there's no need for that: you stick to doing all your little everyday duties, and try and save Phil all the unhappiness you can. [*Enter* CHARLOTTE.]

CHARLOTTE. Ready.

JOHN. Right.

LOWRIE. Yes, I'll do that. I'll save her all the unhappiness I can. Yes, I will. [*Exeunt together, up,* JOHN *and* CHARLOTTE.] [*Goes to window.*] Mind the mill-pond, Chattie; Fly's frisky to-day, he tried to kick me when I fed him, and if he shies when you're mounting—oh, look out!

JOHN. [*off*]. Go carefully, old girl!

CHARLOTTE. [*off*]. All right! We must get a fence put up, it's too close to the door to be safe.

[*Sound of departing horses.* LOWRIE *watches at the window, hesitates, looks round the room, and presently picks up a cushion and goes slowly over to* OWEN, *holding it in front of her with both hands. She stands in front of him holding it near his face. He is quite unconscious of it. He whimpers: his cigarette has gone out.* LOWRIE *puts down the cushion and lights it again for him; picks up the cushion and suddenly collapses with the cushion on his knees, her head on it, sobbing.*]

LOWRIE. Oh, forgive me, Owen darling; you know I love you or I wouldn't be able to do it! It's for you and Phil both I'm going to do it. [OWEN *strokes her hair affectionately, undisturbed.*] Do you think you'll struggle? I wonder if being smothered hurts, if it is very horrible? Oh, Owen, do forgive me! [*She stands up again with the cushion*: *he throws away his cigarette end and whimpers for another.*] Yes, I'll give you another, and then count one, two three and do it. [*She gives him a cigarette; he catches and strokes her hand; she kisses him.*] Owen, I believe you know what I'm saying, and you approve. Oh, you dear! You'll be able to see and hear again in the place I'm sending you to: perhaps you'll be a little boy again among the angels, and there'll be Christ there and all the most wonderful things: there'll be angels, and harps and angels [*she is getting more and more hysterical*] and golden crowns—and one! two!— [*Enter* PHILIPPA *L.*]

PHILIPPA. Lowrie, have you seen my scissors?

[LOWRIE *gasps and drops the cushion.* PHILIPPA *rummages about, not taking much notice of her. As she passes* OWEN, *stops and pats his shoulder.* OWEN *takes her hand, then drops it.*] Isn't he strange? He always wants you, now, Lowrie, to do everything; before, I used to be the only person he would let touch him. I wonder why.

LOWRIE [*still very agitated*]. I don't know.

PHILIPPA. Poor old chap. I'm sure he likes to feel you're by him. [*Wanders out, L.*]

LOWRIE [*taking cloth off the table*]. Supposing she had caught us doing it! What would you have done, Owen? This will be better. It may be good-bye for ever, because you're going to heaven and I'm not sure God won't send me to hell, but I don't care, I don't care—for Phil's sake. Oh, I wonder if I can, now I'm perfectly certain I ought to! Oh, God, help me to do it! I'm very young and weak to wilfully give my soul to be damned, but help me to have strength to do it, for Phil's sake and Chattie's, Amen—Three! [*She twists the cloth round his head and pulls at it madly.* OWEN *flings himself up from his chair and catches her wrist. The cloth falls off his head, but he is gasping, his face red and full of animal terror.* LOWRIE *sinks down behind the chair, but he keeps a hold on her wrist over the back; she springs up wildly; he gropes for her. Suddenly she slips free and lies still on the floor a moment:* OWEN, *whimpering excitedly, begins groping about for her. She gets up and leans against the wall, panting.*] O God! help me! I can't do it! I can't kill him, like in a dream! God, help me! [OWEN *finds the door and gropes for the handle, shaking with terror. It opens, and enter,* PHILIPPA.]

PHILIPPA. I'm sure I left them in here somewhere. Why, what ever's the matter with Owen?

LOWRIE [*in a composed and unnatural voice: her eyes are wide*]. I don't know.

PHILIPPA. Look at your hair! Has he been violent?

LOWRIE [*with a laugh, in a sort of hysterical calm*]. Owen violent! No! Fancy the old dear hurting anyone. [PHILIPPA *takes him by the shoulder, calming him.*] He fell asleep and had a bad dream or something, and jumped up suddenly in a fright.

[PHILIPPA *leads him back to his chair. He sits down still shaking, and when he realizes* PHILIPPA *is preparing to leave him, begins whimpering with terror again.*]

PHILIPPA. What on earth is he so terrified of?

LOWRIE. I can't think.

PHILIPPA [*disengaging* OWEN'S *hands*]. Call me if anything happens.

LOWRIE. All right. I can't think what's the matter with him. [*Exit* PHILIPPA.] It's all over now, I must do it now, or you'd never trust me again and then they might guess. I must do it now, it's not the time to get weak-minded now. But I won't be so silly as to try strength again. [*Glancing at the window.*] The pond! [*She goes to front door, opens it, locks other door; suddenly throws the cloth over his head and springs back. He leaps up, pulling it off, blunders to door L., finds it locked, feels round the wall to the front door, and staggers out.* LOWRIE *slams the door behind him and goes to window.*]

LOWRIE. Pray God he may drown quickly, and not struggle like he did before. [*She kneels up at the window, silent and absolutely still for fully fifteen seconds. Suddenly she gives a half-scream and jumps back, covering her eyes. She turns toward the audience, her eyes covered, still gasping.*] I mustn't scream, I mustn't scream, I mustn't scream. [*She drops her hands and stares about her.*] I mustn't scream, or they'll rescue him. I must wait. [*She stands still a moment, then goes to door L. and unlocks it; rearranges tablecloth.*]

[*Re-enter* PHILIPPA.]

PHILIPPA. They were in my basket after—Hallo, where's he gone?

LOWRIE [*in the same unnaturally calm manner*]. Out. He wanted to go, so I faced him to the paddock and let him.

PHILIPPA. I suppose he's all right. You're sure you got him facing properly?

LOWRIE. Quite. He's all right. I know he's quite all right.

PHILIPPA. Very well, only I'm a bit anxious about him because he seems queer to-day.—Do you think you can wear that frock another winter, dear?

LOWRIE. Frock? Yes, my frock's all right.

PHILIPPA. It's getting very short. I think I had better cut this one of mine down for you.

LOWRIE [*keeping on glancing at the window*]. Yes.

PHILIPPA. Let me measure you. Why, what's the matter? What are you so excited about?

LOWRIE. I'm not excited—I—think he frightened me a bit. Look, there's John and Chattie coming back already.

PHILIPPA. Poor old thing!—I wonder what's wrong with him, he's a lamb generally.

LOWRIE. He didn't mean to—Chattie's leading Fly, and he's stumbling. They must have had a spill, and that's why they have turned back. I do hope they haven't hurt poor Fly.

PHILIPPA [*glancing at the window across the room*]. He doesn't look very bad.

LOWRIE. No, I'm sure he's all right. I'm sure he's quite all right. [*She begins to laugh.*] Silly of me, I don't know what there is to laugh at in that: I know he's quite all right.

JOHN [*off*]. Help! Help!

LOWRIE. What's that?

PHILIPPA. Is one of them hurt?

LOWRIE [*quickly*]. Perhaps that's it.

PHILIPPA [*opens door up, gives a quick cry*]. Stay inside, Lowrie, and don't look out of the window. Promise me you won't look out of the window! [*Exit, closing door. LOWRIE comes forward and stands dry-eyed. Presently shuffling steps and voices outside.*]

PHILIPPA [*off*]. No, don't carry him inside, Lowrie's there.

JOHN [*off*]. Poor kid, she'll be terribly upset.

PHILIPPA [*off*]. Yes, but for his sake we can't be sorry: it was a merciful release to him.

JOHN [*off*]. Amen to that.

PHILIPPA [*off, breaking down*]. Oh, Owen, Owen, my little Owen! Nobody knew him as I did, when you were a beautiful little boy in holland overalls and we used to go exploring up the mill-stream together! I've been a bad sister to you, a cruel sister, I haven't treated you nearly as kindly as I ought, and now he's gone, and I can never do anything for him again! Oh, Owen, I didn't know how much I loved you!

[LOWRIE *suddenly collapses on the floor, weeping loudly.*]

JOHN [*off*]. She's heard! We may as well bring him in.

[*They open the door, and* CHATTIE *and* JOHN, *both quite composed, carry* OWEN'S *body in on a short ladder, his face covered in* JOHN'S *jacket. They bear him straight through the other door.* PHILIPPA *comes to* LOWRIE, *and kneels down beside her.*]

PHILIPPA. You dear, you're all I've got left now: Chattie will get married, and you and I will be all alone. But you mustn't cry for him: he is happy in heaven now. It was God's kind will to him to take him from his suffering. You know, dear, we couldn't wish him to live on as he was; his life was only a misery to him, and it is God's mercy that has released him. Always trust in God, Lowrie, and don't let your own rebellious thoughts interfere with His will. God's purpose is worked out in His own time, and though He may use the weakest of us sometimes as His instruments, it is not for us to anticipate His will: He accomplishes it without any help from us. [*Re-enter* CHARLOTTE *and* JOHN.]

CHARLOTTE. I'm silly, but I can't help crying a bit. Yet I know it's all for the best.—I wish I hadn't talked like that, though: if I'd held my tongue a little longer, there'd have been no need. [*Dabs her eyes.*]

JOHN [*nervously*]. I feel for you, of course, in your bereavement; but we must admit it's all for the best.

PHILIPPA. Yes, John, you're right; it's the best thing for him.

LOWRIE. Phil?

PHILIPPA. Yes, darling.

LOWRIE. I do love you [*pause*]. It was the best thing, wasn't it?

PHILIPPA. Yes.

LOWRIE. Oh, Phil, I do feel awful. Can what's right make you feel awful like that? Did Chattie feel like that?

PHILIPPA. Like what, dear?

LOWRIE. I feel as if God hated me; I don't know why; I can't help it. Oh, I do feel so awful, Phil, I can't bear it.

PHILIPPA. What's the matter?

LOWRIE [*with an effort*]. Nothing. I can't tell you.

PHILIPPA. Do tell me.

LOWRIE. No, I can't: God would never forgive *that*—I *must* bear it. [*Stands up.*] I *will* bear it. I *won't* tell you. [*Walks down stage.*]

CHARLOTTE. What is the matter with her?

PHILIPPA. Sh! She'll tell us presently. She's too wrought up now, don't pay any attention to her.

JOHN. Shall I go now, Chattie? Is there anything else I can do?

PHILIPPA. No, don't go, John; stay a bit.

CHARLOTTE. Phil?

PHILIPPA. Yes?

CHARLOTTE. How did it happen? He doesn't generally go out in the afternoons, and anyhow when he's faced towards the paddock he generally goes straight there. Was he alone?

PHILIPPA. I don't know, Chattie; he was very excited and queer this afternoon. Lowrie started him off all right, she says.

CHARLOTTE. Do you think—? [*She pauses to suggest suicide.* LOWRIE *suddenly screams.*] You'd better make her go to bed, Phil, or she'll be ill.

PHILIPPA. I do *hope* it wasn't that. [LOWRIE *screams again.*]

CHARLOTTE. He knew the pond was there, so he might have done it. You say he seemed very excited and queer.

PHILIPPA. Oh, Chattie, I hope he didn't: I'd be miserable all my life if I thought that was it. Oh, my poor Owen!

JOHN. There's no need to think that, Phil: let's take the charitable view. I can't believe he would be so wicked as to take his own life violently away.

CHARLOTTE. We had better question Lowrie.

PHILIPPA. No, don't, you'll only upset her worse.

CHARLOTTE. It can't be helped.—Lowrie! [LOWRIE *moves up a little, but keeps her face to the audience.*] Did you see him start?

LOWRIE. I saw him walk straight across to the water, and he was kicking with his legs, but he couldn't swim; only he went round and round in circles, and I couldn't look.

PHILIPPA. Lowrie!

JOHN. You saw him fall in?

PHILIPPA. Why didn't you call me? Why didn't you tell me? Oh, Lowrie, we might have saved him!

LOWRIE [*shaking her head*]. I couldn't tell you.

PHILIPPA. Oh, Lowrie, we might!

LOWRIE [*turning*]. No, Pippy dear; you said it was for the best, didn't you? You said he was happier now, and it was God's will: so why should you want to save him?

PHILIPPA. How can you say such wicked things!

LOWRIE. I'll tell you how I can say such wicked things, Pippy. It's because I killed him, that's why! I tried to kill him again and again, but I couldn't, because he was so strong and I was such a weak little fool. If only I had thought of drowning him at first, I could have done it easily, but in the end I had to frighten him, so that he did not know where he was going. I did it for you, Pippy, because I couldn't bear to see him spoiling your life, and Chattie not able to marry, and he living on in misery. I thought he would be glad to die, Pippy, but he wasn't; he hated it, he fought me. I never meant to tell, I meant to keep it secret, so as you and Chattie would be happy and free and not know; and even if God thought I was wrong and sent me to hell, perhaps you would never know. But I'm a little fool, I couldn't bear it, I had to blurt it out, and now it's all no good and you will be unhappy all the same, because you know. [JOHN *steps towards her and deliberately knocks her down.*]

JOHN. Murderer! Murderer! You, to kill your own blind brother! [*She clings to his foot.*] You snake, give up crawling around me! [*Heaves her off his foot.*]

LOWRIE [*very low*]. Phil!

PHILIPPA. I can't speak to you yet, Lowrie. [*Exit hurriedly L.*]

LOWRIE. But I did it for you and Chattie, John. Can't you see it was for Chattie I did it? So as—you—get married?

JOHN. And d'you think I would marry into a murderer's family? D'you think I would marry the sister of a girl what's going to be 'ung?

LOWRIE. Hung!

JOHN. Yes, when I've told the police, they'll come and hang you, Lowrie; and may God have mercy on your soul: though I doubt much if He ought to.

CHARLOTTE. Will you tell?

LOWRIE. I'll go with you, John; I'll go to the police quietly; I'd rather go than wait for them to come and fetch me.

JOHN. You will not! Do you think I want my name dragged into a business like this, a dirty, foul business? You'll stay here! Christ, I'm afraid of the lightning dropping while you're about me! [*Moves to door up:* LOWRIE *follows him.*] Get inside! And don't you even exasperate the Lord by praying to Him. [*Exit:* LOWRIE *buries her face in a chair.*]

CHARLOTTE. John! [*She runs suddenly after him, calling, leaving the door open.*]

LOWRIE. It isn't true! It isn't true! I never did it, I

never! Oh, I know I never did it, I couldn't do, I couldn't
do it. I couldn't kill anything! Oh, Owen! He'll go telling
lies and the police will come and hang me, and it's all a
mistake, a dream, I never did it, I only dreamt it, it's all
a dream! [*Kneels upright, putting her hands together.*]
O God, it's a dream, isn't it? Kind God, let me wake up
now. I've been dreaming long enough. O God, help me to
wake up, and I'll never dare to go to sleep again, never,
never! Oh, let me wake up! [*She bites the back of her hand
and waits a moment, rigid, expectant, with her eyes shut:
then suddenly opens them.*] I'm awake now, say I'm awake
now. Say I dreamt it all about Owen, say I'm in bed; say
he's all right! O God, I'm sure he's all right, I'm sure he's
quite all right, I know he's quite all right—silly of me to
laugh. [*Gets up, looking round the room.*] Owen! Owen!
Where are you? They said you'd be able to hear and see
again where you've gone to: you must hear me, you haven't
died into the blackness, have you? [*She falls by the pool of
water near the door.*] O wicked water, you know you're only
a dream, aren't you? I didn't really see you dripping out of
him—O wicked water, why won't you let me wake up? Owen,
Owen! He's all right, only he can't hear me, and now John
is telling lies, when it was all a dream! O Owen, come and
save me! Owen!

[*She stands stock still, listening: there is silence for five
seconds. LOWRIE runs to the door, opens it: there is nothing
there. She gives a cry of delight, and crooks her arm exactly as before; comes back as if leading him to his chair
by the fire.*]

LOWRIE. I *knew* it was only a dream!

QUICK CURTAIN

THE INTRUDER

(*L'INTRUSE*)

MAURICE MAETERLINCK

TRANSLATED BY JOHN HEARD

Copyright, 1934, by International Pocket Library Corporation

TRANSLATOR'S NOTE

The reader of this play may be struck by the frequent and apparently unnecessary repetition of words and phrases. This is not an oversight on the part of the author, nor a careless rendering by the translator. In many of his plays Maeterlinck deliberately repeats words and short groups of words as a method of enhancing an atmosphere of the supernatural, of horror, of fear, of gloom, of awe. His purpose is similar to that which Poe sought to achieve by his recurring use of the rhyme "ore" in "The Raven". The effect and the success of the technique is nowhere more strikingly illustrated than in "The Intruder", as will be very noticeable if the play is read aloud.

DRAMATIS PERSONAE

THE GRANDFATHER [*he is blind*]
THE FATHER
THE UNCLE
THE THREE DAUGHTERS
THE SISTER OF CHARITY
THE MAID

The Scene is laid in modern times.
A rather dark room in an old country house. Door on the right, door on the left, small door in the corner. At the back of the stage windows with inserts of stained glass in which green is the dominant color, and a glass door leading onto a terrace. A tall Dutch clock stands in one corner. A lamp is burning on the table.

THE THREE DAUGHTERS. Come over here, grandfather. Come over here by the light.

THE GRANDFATHER. It isn't very light here.

THE FATHER. Shall we go out on to the terrace, or shall we stay here indoors?

THE UNCLE. Isn't it wiser to stay here? It rained all the week and the nights are cold and damp.

THE ELDEST DAUGHTER. The stars are out.

THE UNCLE. Oh, the stars! That doesn't mean anything.

THE GRANDFATHER. It's better to stay here. You never can tell what may happen.

THE FATHER. You needn't worry now. She's turned the corner; she's out of danger.

THE GRANDFATHER. I don't believe she's doing as well as . . .

THE FATHER. Why do you say that?

THE GRANDFATHER. Her voice . . . I've heard her voice . . .

THE FATHER. But the doctors tell us not to worry.

THE UNCLE. You know your father-in-law likes to make us worry.

THE GRANDFATHER. I can't see things as well as you do.

THE UNCLE. Then depend on us who can see. She looked well this afternoon. She's sleeping soundly now. We don't propose to spoil the first quiet evening we've had—not unless we have to. There's no need of worrying and so it seems to me we can rest a little, and even laugh a little this evening.

THE FATHER. You're right. Why, it's the first time I've felt at home in my own house among my own family since this terrible child-birth began.

THE UNCLE. As soon as sickness comes into a family it seems as though there were a stranger in the house.

THE FATHER. Yes, and it makes you realize that you can't rely on anyone outside the family.

THE UNCLE. That's very true.

THE GRANDFATHER. Why wasn't I allowed to see my daughter today?

THE UNCLE. You know the doctor wouldn't allow it.

THE GRANDFATHER. I don't know . . . what to think . . .

THE UNCLE. It will do you no good to worry.

THE GRANDFATHER. [*pointing to the door at the left*]. She can't hear us, can she?

THE FATHER. We'll talk quietly. Besides, the door's very heavy, and the nurse is with her. She'd tell us if we made too much noise.

THE GRANDFATHER [*pointing to the door at the right*]. He can't hear us, can he?

THE FATHER. No.

THE GRANDFATHER. Is he asleep?

THE FATHER. Probably.

THE GRANDFATHER. You ought to make sure.

THE UNCLE. In *your* place I should worry more about the child than about your wife. He's several weeks old, and he's hardly moved: he hasn't cried once. He might be made of wax.

THE GRANDFATHER. I think he'll be deaf and perhaps dumb . . . that's what comes of marriages between relatives . . . [*They all remain silent to show their disapproval.*]

THE FATHER. I almost hate him for the suffering he's caused his mother.

THE UNCLE. Oh come; be reasonable! It isn't the poor child's fault. Is he all alone in that room?

THE FATHER. Yes. The doctor doesn't want him to be in his mother's room.

THE UNCLE. Is the nurse with him?

THE FATHER. No. She's gone to her room to rest. She deserves it after these last days. Ursula, go and see if he's asleep.

THE ELDEST DAUGHTER. Yes, father. [*The three sisters go hand in hand into the room at the right.*]

THE FATHER. At what time is sister coming?

THE UNCLE. I think she's coming at about nine o'clock.

THE FATHER. It's after nine now. I wish she'd come. My wife is very anxious to see her tonight.

THE UNCLE. Oh, she'll surely come. Is it the first time she has come here?

THE FATHER. She's never been inside the house.

THE UNCLE. It's very difficult for her to leave her convent.

THE FATHER. Will she come alone?

THE UNCLE. I think one of the nuns will come with her. They are not allowed to go out alone.

THE FATHER. But she is the Mother Superior.

THE UNCLE. The rule applies to everyone.

THE GRANDFATHER. Aren't you worried?

THE UNCLE. Why should we be worried? Let's not go over all that again. There is nothing to worry about.

THE GRANDFATHER. Is your sister older than you?

THE UNCLE. She's the eldest of the family.

THE GRANDFATHER. I don't know what troubles me; I'm not easy . . . I wish . . . your sister were here.

THE UNCLE. She'll come. She promised to come.

THE GRANDFATHER. I wish this evening were over. [*The three sisters return.*]

THE FATHER. Is he asleep?

THE ELDEST DAUGHTER. Yes, father, he's sound asleep.

THE UNCLE. What shall we do while we're waiting?

THE GRANDFATHER. Waiting for what?

THE UNCLE. Waiting for my sister.

THE FATHER. Can't you see anyone coming, Ursula?

THE ELDEST DAUGHTER. [*at the window*]. No, father; no one.

THE FATHER. No one coming up the avenue? Can you see down the avenue?

THE ELDEST DAUGHTER. Yes, father, I can see. The

moon is up; and I can see down as far as the cypress trees.

THE GRANDFATHER. Can't you see anyone coming up the avenue, Ursula?

THE ELDEST DAUGHTER. No one, grandfather.

THE UNCLE. How is the weather?

THE ELDEST DAUGHTER. The weather's fine. Can't you hear the nightingales singing?

THE UNCLE. Yes, I can hear them.

THE ELDEST DAUGHTER. A little wind is blowing along the avenue.

THE GRANDFATHER. A little wind along the avenue, Ursula? Did you say a little wind?

THE ELDEST DAUGHTER. Yes, the trees are trembling a little.

THE UNCLE. I'm surprised my sister hasn't come yet.

THE GRANDFATHER. I can't hear the nightingales any longer, Ursula.

THE ELDEST DAUGHTER. I think someone has come into the garden, grandfather.

THE GRANDFATHER. Who has come into the garden?

THE ELDEST DAUGHTER. I don't know. I can't see anyone . . .

THE UNCLE. . . . Because there's nobody there.

THE ELDEST DAUGHTER. Someone must have come into the garden. The nightingales have all stopped singing . . . stopped suddenly.

THE GRANDFATHER. But I can't hear any footsteps.

THE ELDEST DAUGHTER. Someone must be passing very close to the pond. All the swans are frightened.

THE SECOND DAUGHTER. And the fish jumped, too.

THE FATHER. Can't you see anyone?

THE ELDEST DAUGHTER. No, father; no one.

THE FATHER. But the pond is in the full moonlight.

THE ELDEST DAUGHTER. Yes, I know. I see that the swans are frightened.

THE UNCLE. It must be my sister who frightened them. She probably came in by the little gate.

THE FATHER. I can't understand why the dogs don't bark.

THE ELDEST DAUGHTER. I can see the watch dog crouching at the very back of his kennel. The swans are all swimming toward the other shore.

THE UNCLE. They're afraid of my sister. I'll go and see. [*He calls out.*] Sister—Sister—Is that you? . . . There's no one there.

THE SECOND DAUGHTER. I'm sure someone must have come into the garden. Listen . . . Wait.

THE UNCLE. She'd surely have answered me.

THE GRANDFATHER. Aren't the nightingales singing again?

THE SECOND DAUGHTER. I can't hear a single one.

THE GRANDFATHER. I can't hear a sound . . . not a sound . . .

THE FATHER. It's as silent as death.

THE GRANDFATHER. It must have been a stranger that frightened the nightingales. A member of the household wouldn't frighten them.

THE ELDEST DAUGHTER. There's one on the big weeping willow. He's flown away . . .

THE UNCLE. What's the trouble now? Are you going to let the nightingales frighten you?

THE GRANDFATHER. Are the windows all open, Ursula?

THE ELDEST DAUGHTER. The glass door is open, grandfather.

THE GRANDFATHER. I feel a cold draft coming into the room.

THE SECOND DAUGHTER. There's a little wind in the garden, grandfather. The rose petals are falling, falling . . .

THE FATHER. Well, Ursula, shut the door; it's late.

THE ELDEST DAUGHTER. Yes, father . . . [*She pushes*

the door.] . . . I can't shut the door . . . [*Her sisters help her.*]

THE TWO OTHER DAUGHTERS. We can't shut the door . . .

THE GRANDFATHER. Who's at the door? Why can't you shut the door?

THE UNCLE. Don't say that in such a voice. I'll help the girls shut it.

THE SECOND DAUGHTER. We can't quite close it.

THE UNCLE. It's the dampness. Now! Let's all push together. Something must be caught between the hinges.

THE FATHER. The carpenter can attend to it tomorrow.

THE GRANDFATHER. Is the carpenter coming tomorrow?

THE SECOND DAUGHTER. Yes, grandfather, he's coming to work in the cellar.

THE GRANDFATHER. I suppose he'll make a noise.

THE THIRD DAUGHTER. I'll tell him to work quietly. [*Suddenly the noise of a scythe being whetted is heard outside.*]

THE GRANDFATHER [*starting*]. Oh!

THE UNCLE. What's that?

THE ELDEST DAUGHTER. I'm not sure. I think it's the gardener. I can't see very well; he's in the shadow of the house.

THE FATHER. It's the gardener getting ready to mow.

THE UNCLE. Getting ready to mow . . . ? At night?

THE FATHER. Tomorrow is Sunday, isn't it? Yes, surely . . . I noticed that the grass was very long about the house.

THE GRANDFATHER. His scythe seems to make a great deal of noise.

THE ELDEST DAUGHTER. He's mowing very close to the house.

THE GRANDFATHER. Can you see him, Ursula?

THE ELDEST DAUGHTER. No, grandfather. He's in the shadow.

THE GRANDFATHER. His scythe seems to make a great deal of noise . . .

THE THIRD DAUGHTER. That's because your ears are very sharp, grandfather.

THE GRANDFATHER. I'm afraid he'll wake my daughter.

THE UNCLE. Why, we can scarcely hear him.

THE GRANDFATHER. I can hear him as clearly as though he were mowing here in this room.

THE UNCLE. She won't hear him—don't worry.

THE FATHER. The lamp doesn't seem to burn very well tonight.

THE UNCLE. It needs oil.

THE FATHER. I saw them filling it this morning. It's burned badly ever since we shut the window.

THE UNCLE. I think the chimney's smoked.

THE FATHER. It will burn better bye and bye.

THE SECOND DAUGHTER. Grandfather's asleep. He hasn't slept for three nights.

THE FATHER. He's been worrying.

THE UNCLE. He always worries unnecessarily. There are times when he simply refuses to be sensible.

THE FATHER. Well, it's excusable at his age.

THE UNCLE. God knows how *we'll* be at his age.

THE FATHER. He's nearly eighty.

THE UNCLE. A man has a right to be queer at eighty.

THE FATHER. We may be even queerer when we get to be his age.

THE UNCLE. You never can tell what will happen. He *is* strange at times.

THE FATHER. He's like all blind people.

THE UNCLE. They think too much.

THE FATHER. Yes . . . They have too much time to kill.

THE UNCLE. They have nothing else to do.

THE FATHER. And no amusements . . .

THE UNCLE. It must be terrible.

THE FATHER. I suppose people become accustomed to it.

THE UNCLE. I can't imagine it.

THE FATHER. They're certainly to be pitied.

THE UNCLE. Not to know where you are: not to know where you came from; not to know where you are going ... not to be able to tell noon from midnight, summer from winter ... and always in the dark ... always in the dark ... I'd rather die! Is it incurable?

THE FATHER. It seems so.

THE UNCLE. He isn't stone blind, is he?

THE FATHER. He can just make out a very bright light.

THE UNCLE. Let's take jolly good care of *our* poor eyes.

THE FATHER. He often has strange ideas.

THE UNCLE. Yes, and at times they're not exactly cheerful.

THE FATHER. He says just what he thinks.

THE UNCLE. But he wasn't that way ... before ... was he?

THE FATHER. No, he used to be as sensible as the rest of us. He never said queer things. To be sure, Ursula encourages him too much; she answers all his questions.

THE UNCLE. Better not to answer him. It's no kindness to him. [*Ten o'clock strikes.*]

THE GRANDFATHER [*waking*]. Am I facing the glass door?

THE SECOND DAUGHTER. Did you have a good nap, grandfather?

THE GRANDFATHER. Am I facing the glass door?

THE ELDEST DAUGHTER. Yes, grandfather.

THE GRANDFATHER. And there is nobody at the glass door?

THE ELDEST DAUGHTER. Why no, grandfather. I don't see anyone.

THE GRANDFATHER. It seemed to me someone was waiting . . . Hasn't anyone come, Ursula?

THE ELDEST DAUGHTER. No one has come.

THE GRANDFATHER [*to the Father and the Uncle*]. And your sister hasn't come?

THE UNCLE. It's too late. She won't come now. It's not kind of her.

THE FATHER. I'm beginning to be worried about her. [*There is a sound as of someone entering the basement of the house.*]

THE UNCLE. There she is! Did you hear her?

THE FATHER. Yes. Someone came in by the basement.

THE UNCLE. It must be sister. I recognized her step.

THE GRANDFATHER. I heard someone walking slowly . . . very slowly.

THE FATHER. She came in very quietly.

THE UNCLE. She knows there's sickness.

THE GRANDFATHER. I don't hear anything now.

THE UNCLE. She'll be up directly. Someone will tell her we are here.

THE FATHER. I'm glad she's come.

THE UNCLE. I was sure she would come tonight.

THE GRANDFATHER. She's very slow coming up.

THE UNCLE. It must be she.

THE FATHER. We aren't expecting anyone else.

THE GRANDFATHER. I can't hear a sound in the basement.

THE FATHER. I'll call the maid and we'll find out what it's all about. [*He pulls the bell cord.*]

THE GRANDFATHER. I can hear a noise on the stairs.

THE FATHER. It's the maid coming upstairs.

THE GRANDFATHER. I think there is someone with her.

THE FATHER. It must be the maid who's making all the noise.

THE GRANDFATHER. I think there is someone with her . . .

THE FATHER. She's getting too fat. I think she's developing dropsy.

THE UNCLE. You'd better get rid of her. The next thing you know you'll be saddled with her for life.

THE GRANDFATHER. I hear your sister's step.

THE FATHER. All I can hear is the maid.

THE GRANDFATHER. It's your sister . . . it's your sister. [*Someone knocks at the smaller door.*]

THE UNCLE. She's knocking at the door of the back-stairs.

THE FATHER. I'll open the door myself. That little door makes so much noise. It's only used when someone wants to come into the room without being seen. [*He opens the door. The* MAID *stands just outside.*] Where are you?

THE MAID. Here, sir.

THE GRANDFATHER. Is your sister at the door?

THE UNCLE. Only the maid.

THE FATHER. Only the maid. [*To the* MAID] Who came into the house?

THE MAID. Into the house, sir?

THE FATHER. Yes, someone just came into the house.

THE MAID. No one came in, sir.

THE GRANDFATHER. Who's breathing so hard? Who's breathing so hard?

THE UNCLE. It's the maid. She's out of breath.

THE GRANDFATHER. Is she crying?

THE UNCLE. Crying? Why no. Why should she be crying?

THE FATHER [*to the* MAID]. Didn't someone come in, just now?

THE MAID. No, sir.

THE FATHER. But we heard the door open.

THE MAID. I just shut the door, sir. Perhaps you heard that.

THE FATHER. Was the door open?

THE MAID. Yes, sir.

THE FATHER. Why was it open at this time?

THE MAID. I don't know, sir. I shut it myself, earlier.

THE FATHER. Well, then, who opened it?

THE MAID. I don't know, sir. Someone must have gone out after I'd shut the door.

THE FATHER. You must be more careful. There, now, don't push the door open! You know it squeaks.

THE MAID. I'm not pushing the door, sir.

THE FATHER. Yes, you are. You're pushing it as if you wanted to come into the room.

THE MAID. But, sir, I'm not within three feet of the door.

THE FATHER. Don't speak so loud.

THE GRANDFATHER. Has someone put out the light?

THE ELDEST DAUGHTER. Why no, grandfather.

THE GRANDFATHER. It seems to have grown dark all of a sudden.

THE FATHER [*to the* MAID]. You can go down again; and don't make so much noise on the stairs.

THE MAID. But, sir, I didn't make any noise on the stairs.

THE FATHER. I tell you you made a noise. Go down quietly. You'll wake my wife.

THE MAID. Very well, sir, but it wasn't me made any noise.

THE FATHER. If anyone calls, say we are out.

THE UNCLE. Yes, say we are out.

THE GRANDFATHER [*starting*]. You mustn't say that . . . not that . . .

THE FATHER. . . . Except, of course, my sister or the doctor . . .

THE UNCLE. When is the doctor coming?

THE FATHER. Very likely not until midnight. [*He shuts the door. Eleven o'clock strikes.*]

THE GRANDFATHER. Did she come into the room?

THE FATHER. Who?

THE GRANDFATHER. The maid.

THE FATHER. Why no, she went downstairs.

THE GRANDFATHER. I thought she came in and sat down at the table.

THE UNCLE. Who? The maid?

THE GRANDFATHER. Yes.

THE UNCLE. That would be the last straw.

THE GRANDFATHER. Didn't someone come into the room?

THE FATHER. No! No! No one came into the room.

THE GRANDFATHER. And your sister isn't here?

THE UNCLE. My sister didn't come—don't you remember? What are you thinking about?

THE GRANDFATHER. You are trying to deceive me.

THE UNCLE. Deceive you?

THE GRANDFATHER. Ursula, tell me the truth! For God's sake, tell me the truth!

THE ELDEST DAUGHTER. What is it, grandfather? What is it?

THE GRANDFATHER. Something has happened . . . Something has happened . . . I am sure my daughter is worse.

THE UNCLE. You're imagining things.

THE GRANDFATHER. You see! You won't tell me! I can see something has happened . . .

THE UNCLE. Well, if that's the case, your eyes are better than ours.

THE GRANDFATHER. Ursula, tell me the truth.

THE ELDEST DAUGHTER. But, grandfather, we *are* telling you the truth.

THE GRANDFATHER. Your voice isn't natural.

THE FATHER. You frightened her.

THE GRANDFATHER. And *your* voice is different, too.

THE FATHER. You're crazy! [*The* FATHER *and the* UNCLE *make signs at each other to indicate that the* GRANDFATHER *is crazy.*]

THE GRANDFATHER. I can hear that you are frightened.

THE FATHER. Why should we be frightened?

THE GRANDFATHER. Why are you trying to deceive me?

THE UNCLE. Who's trying to deceive you?

THE GRANDFATHER. Why have you put out the light?

THE UNCLE. No one has put out the light. The room is just as light now as it has been.

THE ELDEST DAUGHTER. I *do* think the lamp is dimmer.

THE FATHER. I can see perfectly well. I don't see any difference.

THE GRANDFATHER. And I can see pin-wheels everywhere. Girls, tell me what has happened, tell me, for God's sake! You can see! I'm here all alone in the dark . . . the everlasting dark. I don't know who sits down beside me; I don't know what goes on three feet away . . . Why were you whispering just now?

THE FATHER. No one was whispering.

THE GRANDFATHER. You were whispering . . . over . . . there . . . by the door.

THE FATHER. We weren't. You heard everything I said.

THE GRANDFATHER. Didn't you let someone into the room?

THE FATHER. No, I tell you! No one came into the room!

THE GRANDFATHER. Was it your sister—or a priest? . . . You mustn't try to deceive me. Ursula, you'll tell me. Who came in?

THE ELDEST DAUGHTER. No one, grandfather.

THE GRANDFATHER. Don't try to deceive me—I know what I know—how many are we here?

THE SECOND DAUGHTER. There are six of us sitting at the table.

THE GRANDFATHER. Are you all sitting at the table?

THE ELDEST DAUGHTER. Yes, grandfather.

THE GRANDFATHER. Are you there, Paul?

THE FATHER. Yes.

THE GRANDFATHER. Are you there, Oliver?

THE UNCLE. Yes, yes, yes. I'm here, in my regular chair. Are you joking?

THE GRANDFATHER. Are you there, Genevieve?

ONE OF THE DAUGHTERS. Yes, grandfather.

THE GRANDFATHER. Are you there, Gertrude?

ANOTHER DAUGHTER. Yes, grandfather.

THE GRANDFATHER. And you, Ursula, are you here?

THE ELDEST DAUGHTER. Yes, grandfather, here, sitting beside you.

THE GRANDFATHER. And who is sitting over there?

THE ELDEST DAUGHTER. Where, grandfather? Over there? There is no one over there.

THE GRANDFATHER. There . . . there . . . right amongst us.

THE ELDEST DAUGHTER. But there isn't *anyone* over there.

THE FATHER. Can't we make you understand that there is no one over there?

THE GRANDFATHER. Oh, you can't see . . . you can't see . . . you . . .

THE UNCLE. Are you joking?

THE GRANDFATHER. I am *not* joking; I assure you I have no desire to joke.

THE UNCLE. Well then; believe what people who *can* see, tell you.

THE GRANDFATHER [*doubtfully*]. It seemed to me . . . it seemed to me that someone was sitting over there . . . I don't believe I shall live much longer now . . .

THE UNCLE. Why should we try to deceive you? What good would it do us?

THE FATHER. We'd have to tell you the truth in the end.

THE UNCLE. What would be the use of trying to fool each other?

THE FATHER. It wouldn't be long before you found out.

THE GRANDFATHER. I wish I were at home . . .

THE FATHER. But you *are* at home.

THE UNCLE. Aren't we all at home here?

THE FATHER. You aren't exactly among strangers, are you?

THE UNCLE. *You* are strange tonight.

THE GRANDFATHER. And yet, all of you seem so strange to me.

THE FATHER. Is there anything you'd like?

THE GRANDFATHER. I don't know what's the trouble . . . I don't know . . .

THE UNCLE. Would you like something to drink?

THE ELDEST DAUGHTER. What would you like, grandfather? Tell me, what would you like?

THE GRANDFATHER. Let me hold your little hands, dear.

ALL THE DAUGHTERS. Yes, grandfather.

THE GRANDFATHER. Why are you all trembling—all three of you?

THE ELDEST DAUGHTER. Only a little bit.

THE GRANDFATHER. I think all of you are pale.

THE ELDEST DAUGHTER. It's late, grandfather, and we're tired.

THE FATHER. You girls ought to go to bed, and grandfather would do well to rest a little, too.

THE GRANDFATHER. I couldn't sleep tonight . . . not tonight . . .

THE UNCLE. We'll wait for the doctor.

THE GRANDFATHER. You can tell me the truth. I'm ready.

THE UNCLE. But there's nothing to tell you . . .

THE GRANDFATHER. Well, then . . . I don't know . . . I don't know . . .

THE UNCLE. And I tell you there is nothing at all the matter . . . nothing.

THE GRANDFATHER. I'd like to see my poor daughter . . .

THE FATHER. But you know it's impossible. She mustn't be disturbed unnecessarily.

THE UNCLE. You can see her tomorrow.

THE GRANDFATHER. I don't hear a sound in her room.

THE UNCLE. I'm glad of it; I should be worried if I heard anything.

THE GRANDFATHER [*very slowly*]. It's a long time since I've seen my daughter. Yesterday evening I took her hands . . . and I couldn't see her. I don't know what's happening to her. I don't know how she looks any longer . . . I wouldn't know her face, now . . . She must have changed during these last weeks . . . I could feel the little bones in her hands . . . There's nothing now but darkness between you and her and me . . . This isn't life . . . This isn't living . . . You are all of you standing there with open eyes, staring at my dead ones,—and not one of you pities me. No, not one of you . . . I don't know what's the trouble with me . . . No one ever says what they ought to say . . . Everything's so terrifying when you think about it . . . when you think . . . Why aren't any of you talking?

THE UNCLE. What do you want us to talk about? You won't believe us.

THE GRANDFATHER. You are afraid of giving yourselves away.

THE FATHER. Oh, really! Do be sensible, please.

THE GRANDFATHER. People have been hiding something from me for a long time. Something's happened in this house . . . I'm beginning to understand . . . You have been deceiving me too long . . . ha, ha, you thought I'd never find out. You know; there are times when I can see better than you can . . . When I am not as blind as you. Don't you suppose I've heard you whispering . . . whispering . . . day after day . . . as if you were in a room with a corpse

. . . I don't dare tell you what I know tonight . . . I'll know the truth . . . I was waiting for you to tell me the truth, but I've known the truth . . . Yes, I have known the truth a long time . . . Yes, a long time . . . in spite of you . . . and now I can feel that you are all as pale as corpses.

THE THREE DAUGHTERS. Grandfather! Grandfather! What's the trouble?

THE GRANDFATHER. I'm not talking of you, girls. It's not of you I'm talking. I know you'd tell me the truth if the others weren't there, around you. And then, besides, I'm sure they're deceiving you, too. You'll see, you'll see. Don't you suppose I hear you sobbing—all three of you?

THE UNCLE. I'm not going to stay here any longer.

THE FATHER. Is my wife really worse?

THE GRANDFATHER. You mustn't try to deceive me any longer. I know the truth now . . . know it better than you do.

THE UNCLE. Oh! Have it your own way. After all, we're not blind, you know.

THE FATHER. Do you want to go into your daughter's room? There's some mistake here, and it's time to clear it up, once and for all. Well, do you want to go?

THE GRANDFATHER. No, not now . . . not yet . . .

THE UNCLE. There! Do you see how unreasonable you are?

THE GRANDFATHER. There are things a man never can explain, no matter how long he lives . . . Who is making that noise?

THE ELDEST DAUGHTER. The lamp's flickering, grandfather.

THE GRANDFATHER. Something must be making the lamp flicker.

THE ELDEST DAUGHTER. It's the wind that makes it flicker—the cold draft makes it flicker.

THE UNCLE. There isn't any wind, and there isn't any draft. The windows are all closed.

THE ELDEST DAUGHTER. I think the lamp's going out.

THE FATHER. There's no more oil.

THE SECOND DAUGHTER. It's gone out.

THE FATHER. We can't sit here in the dark.

THE GRANDFATHER. Why not? It makes no difference to me.

THE FATHER. There's a light in my wife's room.

THE UNCLE. We'll fetch a light bye and bye when the doctor comes.

THE FATHER. It isn't so dark after all; it's quite light outside.

THE GRANDFATHER. Is it light outside?

THE FATHER. Lighter than it is here.

THE UNCLE. Oh, well, I rather like talking in the dark.

THE FATHER. So do I. [*Silence.*]

THE GRANDFATHER. It seems to me the clock is very noisy.

THE ELDEST DAUGHTER. That's because no one is talking, grandfather.

THE GRANDFATHER. But why are you all so silent?

THE UNCLE. What do you expect us to talk about? You're impossible this evening!

THE GRANDFATHER. Is the room very dark?

THE UNCLE. It's not so very dark. [*Silence.*]

THE GRANDFATHER. I don't feel very well . . . Ursula, open the window a little.

THE FATHER. Yes, open the window a little. I'd like a little air. [URSULA *opens the window.*]

THE UNCLE. I'm sure we've stayed shut up here too long without any air.

THE GRANDFATHER. Is the window open, Ursula?

THE ELDEST DAUGHTER. Yes, grandfather; wide open.

THE GRANDFATHER. It doesn't seem as though it were open. I can't hear a sound from outside.

THE ELDEST DAUGHTER. No, there isn't a sound.

THE FATHER. It's extraordinarily quiet.

THE ELDEST DAUGHTER. I believe one could hear angels walking.

THE UNCLE. That's one reason I don't like the country.

THE GRANDFATHER. I wish I could hear some sound . . . What time is it, Ursula?

THE ELDEST DAUGHTER. Nearly midnight, grandfather. [*The* UNCLE *begins to pace the floor.*]

THE GRANDFATHER. Who's walking about?

THE UNCLE. It's I. It's I. Don't be afraid. I've got to stretch my legs. [*Silence*].

I'm going to sit down again. I can't see where I'm going. [*Silence*].

THE GRANDFATHER. I'd like to be somewhere else . . . yes, somewhere else . . .

THE ELDEST DAUGHTER. Where would you like to go, grandfather?

THE GRANDFATHER. I don't know . . . Into some other room . . . Any other room . . . Anywhere.

THE FATHER. Well, where do you want to go?

THE UNCLE. It's too late to go anywhere now. [*Silence. They sit about the table without moving.*]

THE GRANDFATHER. What do I hear, Ursula?

THE ELDEST DAUGHTER. Nothing, grandfather. Only the leaves falling. [*She listens.*] Yes, the leaves are falling onto the terrace.

THE GRANDFATHER. Shut the window, Ursula.

THE ELDEST DAUGHTER. Yes, grandfather. [*She shuts the window and sits down again.*]

THE GRANDFATHER. I'm cold. [*Silence. The three sisters embrace each other.*] What do I hear?

THE FATHER. The girls kissing each other.

THE UNCLE. They're very pale this evening. [*Silence.*]

THE GRANDFATHER. What do I hear, Ursula?

THE ELDEST DAUGHTER. Nothing, grandfather. I folded my hands. [*Silence.*]

THE GRANDFATHER. What's that I hear, Ursula? What's that I hear?

ANOTHER DAUGHTER. I don't know, grandfather. Maybe you hear my sisters. They're trembling.

THE GRANDFATHER. I'm afraid, children. I'm afraid, too. [*A shaft of moonlight comes through one corner of the window and throws a few vague and ghostly streaks of light here and there throughout the room. Midnight strikes, and at the last stroke one seems to hear, very faintly, the sound of someone standing up hurriedly.*]

THE GRANDFATHER [*in great terror*]. Who stood up? Who stood up?

THE UNCLE. No one stood up.

THE FATHER. I didn't stand up.

THE THREE DAUGHTERS. Nor I. Nor I. Nor I.

THE GRANDFATHER. Someone stood up from the table.

THE UNCLE. Light the light. [*Suddenly one hears a wail of terror in the child's room on the right. The wail continues in growing terror until the end of the scene.*]

THE FATHER. Listen! The child!

THE UNCLE. It never cried before!

THE FATHER. Let's see what has happened.

THE UNCLE. The light. Where's the light!

[*Footsteps are heard running hurriedly in the room on the left, then a death-like stillness. They all listen in terrified silence until the door of the room on the left opens slowly. The room is flooded with light from outside. The* SISTER OF CHARITY *stands on the threshold in her black robes, making the sign of the cross to announce the death of the* MOTHER. *They understand, and after a moment of hesitation and horror silently file into the room of death while the* UNCLE, *standing by the door, draws back politely to let the three girls pass. The blind man, left alone, gets up and fumbles about, tapping his way around the table.*]

THE GRANDFATHER. Where are you going? Where are you going? . . . They've left me alone . . . alone.

CURTAIN